T0093960

Practical User Research

Everything You Need to Know to Integrate User Research to Your Product Development

Dr. Emmanuelle Savarit

Apress®

Practical User Research

Dr. Emmanuelle Savarit
London, UK

ISBN-13 (pbk): 978-1-4842-5595-7   ISBN-13 (electronic): 978-1-4842-5596-4
https://doi.org/10.1007/978-1-4842-5596-4

Copyright © 2020 by Dr. Emmanuelle Savarit

This work is subject to copyright. All rights are reserved by the Publisher, whether the whole or part of the material is concerned, specifically the rights of translation, reprinting, reuse of illustrations, recitation, broadcasting, reproduction on microfilms or in any other physical way, and transmission or information storage and retrieval, electronic adaptation, computer software, or by similar or dissimilar methodology now known or hereafter developed.

Trademarked names, logos, and images may appear in this book. Rather than use a trademark symbol with every occurrence of a trademarked name, logo, or image we use the names, logos, and images only in an editorial fashion and to the benefit of the trademark owner, with no intention of infringement of the trademark.

The use in this publication of trade names, trademarks, service marks, and similar terms, even if they are not identified as such, is not to be taken as an expression of opinion as to whether or not they are subject to proprietary rights.

While the advice and information in this book are believed to be true and accurate at the date of publication, neither the authors nor the editors nor the publisher can accept any legal responsibility for any errors or omissions that may be made. The publisher makes no warranty, express or implied, with respect to the material contained herein.

Managing Director, Apress Media LLC: Welmoed Spahr
Acquisitions Editor: Louise Corrigan
Development Editor: James Markham
Coordinating Editor: Nancy Chen

Cover designed by eStudioCalamar

Cover image designed by Freepik (www.freepik.com)

Distributed to the book trade worldwide by Springer Science+Business Media New York, 1 New York Plaza, New York, NY 10004. Phone 1-800-SPRINGER, fax (201) 348-4505, e-mail orders-ny@springer-sbm.com, or visit www.springeronline.com. Apress Media, LLC is a California LLC and the sole member (owner) is Springer Science + Business Media Finance Inc (SSBM Finance Inc). SSBM Finance Inc is a **Delaware** corporation.

For information on translations, please e-mail rights@apress.com, or visit www.apress.com/rights-permissions.

Apress titles may be purchased in bulk for academic, corporate, or promotional use. eBook versions and licenses are also available for most titles. For more information, reference our Print and eBook Bulk Sales web page at www.apress.com/bulk-sales.

Any source code or other supplementary material referenced by the author in this book is available to readers on GitHub via the book's product page, located at www.apress.com/9781484255957. For more detailed information, please visit www.apress.com/source-code.

Printed on acid-free paper

I would like to dedicate this book to Charles Goodwin, Marjorie H. Goodwin, and Emanuel Schegloff.

Table of Contents

About the Author

Dr. Emmanuelle Savarit has a strong academic background and has worked closely with leaders in qualitative research methodology at the University of California – Los Angeles (UCLA). She has worked on a freelance basis with several companies in the Silicon Valley area and has worked at the University of Technology of Compiègne (UTC) in France, one of the leading French engineering universities, as well as the Clinical Safety Research Unit at Imperial College, London. In 2010 Emmanuelle left academia and decided to focus exclusively on her consulting work through Analyse-Concept Ltd, which specializes in user research. She has provided services in the private sector for companies such as Betfair, HSBC, Thompson Reuters, Graze, Odigeo, Adecco, and Education First, as well as in the public sector for the Home Office, Department for Work and Pension, and Department for Education. Emmanuelle is frequently invited to speak at conferences around the world and organizes workshops to upskill and train others to become user researchers. You can find her on Twitter (@eSavarit) and find out more about her through her website (www.emmanuelle-savarit.com).

About the Technical Reviewers

François-Denis Gonthier is a graduate of the Université de Sherbrooke computer science program. His first job was for a startup company delivering cryptographic software using open source technologies. From this point on, he has never strayed far from the Linux and open source world, without really settling in a single area. He went from programming front ends in JavaScript and HTML 5.0 to coding website backends using Java, J2EE, JSF, or plain old Unix daemons. The cool Web 2.0 kids would call this being a "full stack developer." Nowadays, he mostly works on embedded Android projects and writes JavaScript running on Node.js when he's not doing that.

Alexander Chinedu Nnakwue has a background in mechanical engineering from the University of Ibadan, Nigeria, and has been a front-end developer for more than three years working on both web and mobile technologies. He also has experience as a technical author, writer, and reviewer. He enjoys programming for the Web, and occasionally, you can also find him playing soccer. He was born in Benin City and is currently based in Lagos, Nigeria.

Acknowledgments

This book would not have been possible without the generosity and support of a number of people.

First, I am deeply thankful to all the participants who allowed me to carry out research with them over the years. Without them, it would have been impossible to develop these insights.

I am also grateful to all my fellow user (UX) researchers who worked with me over the last ten years.

I would also like to say that without my loved ones, this book would never have been completed; a big thank-you to them for their patience, support, and understanding.

CHAPTER 1

Introduction to User Research

This introductory chapter defines *user research* and aims to give you some background information on the origins of the term to put it in better context. We'll then review the roles and skill sets of user researchers, taking into consideration their level of experience, followed by an overview of how to become a user researcher today and the training available for that role. Finally, we'll look at the benefits of user research and why and when companies should integrate it into their product development life cycle.

The Origins of User Research

It is not easy to come up with a common definition of what *user research* (UR) is, especially when people use trendy words such as *user experience* (UX) without knowing what roles are attached to either term. It certainly confounds things when linking the role of user experience researchers with the role of user experience designers. Even if user researchers work closely with UX designers, there are some significant differences between the two, since the former is creative and the latter scientific. Therefore, it's important to make a clear distinction and define *user research* in the context of this book.

User research consists of putting an end user's needs at the center of the researcher's investigation. The user is the person who is currently or will be using your product and your service. For example, if you are developing an app for children, a child should be the focal point of the research, along with the parents as they are the money holders. Or, if you are looking at a property website, the user research will identify who the users are and try to understand their behavior and their motivation. User research also means putting new concepts, design, or tools in front of users and evaluating how they interact with them. This definition reflects what we are doing currently as user researchers, and

© Emmanuelle Savarit 2020
E. Savarit, *Practical User Research*, https://doi.org/10.1007/978-1-4842-5596-4_1

it reduces any confusion between research (UR) and design (UX). With this in mind, for perspective, it's important to provide a snapshot of where user research originated.

With the evolution of new technology, the democratization of computers and mobile/smartphones, and the influence of social media, user research today is at the center of the development of sites, apps, software, and platforms, especially if businesses want to provide a user-centered product.

To get a better understanding of what user research is, it is essential to understand the context around its evolution. Many disciplines, such as ergonomics, human and computer interaction, human factor, usability, human behavior, cognitive psychology, social psychology, and anthropology, have influenced user research.

All these disciplines are still playing an essential part in the development of user research as a field. I will give some background that will show how all these disciplines help in the development of user research as a field.

Ergonomics

Ergonomics emerged in the 1940s with the development of complex engineering equipment, especially in the aeronautics and defense sectors. Ergonomics developed during and just after the World War II. The trigger was when soldiers came back from operations with severe injuries, not because of the fighting itself but because of the consequences of using military equipment (see Figure 1-1).

Figure 1-1. *Military equipment often had its consequences*

The effect of the damages had some severe impacts, not only because the soldiers required medical treatment but because the military was losing its resources (injured soldiers could not go back to the battle). In addition, some soldiers long-term effects and couldn't remain in the army at all.

Solutions were needed to reduce the risk of injuries. A new form of work emerged that led to redesigning equipment and taking into consideration the operator's (user's) physiology as well the cognitive effort required to operate the equipment.

Before the 1940s, the engineers created equipment based on technical mechanisms and military requirements. The aim of developing the technology was to meet military and strategic war needs.

The only way to prevent injuries, or limit long-term physical damage, was to have a better understanding of the users and how they would be operating the equipment. The engineers needed the support of physiologists and psychologists to help them to understand how the soldier was going to use their equipment.

Engineers had to start taking a broader picture in the development of their equipment, which means that they had to understand the people who would be using it.

It is not always easy to make engineers understand that, eventually, someone is going to use the product/equipment that they have developed. Several years ago, I was teaching some user research classes to engineers at the University of Technology of Compiegne. What surprised me was that the engineers concentrated on the mechanism and functionalities; they did not anticipate at all the people who would be using their tools.

KNOW YOUR AUDIENCE

The other day, I was trying to set up the timer of my underfloor heating thermostat. The instructions were like a foreign language to me. I went to the Web and found a video. The problem was that the instructions on the video were so fast. It was almost assuming that I knew already what to do. I had to pause the video and play it again several times while writing the necessary instructions on a sticky note.

The same thing happens when we try to build furniture. The instructions take a mechanical perspective. How many times do you have to turn the instructions? Did the person who created the guidance think about who would need to read it? We should say thank you to Ikea, which makes furniture-building instructions simple.

An ergonomist generally has a background in engineering or psychological sciences. Over the years, ergonomists have developed methods and theories to understand the interaction between man and machine.

Ergonomists help develop sophisticated military tools and inform engineers about how real users will be using their equipment. They also need to understand how professionals will be using them in real situations. The work of ergonomists also help to identify the reasons for poor performance. Their role is to investigate using scientific research methods, collect data, analyze it, and provide an evidence-based recommendation to engineers. That will help them to improve their product and equipment.

Some physiologists and psychologists also started developing their discipline and calling it *human factor*. Their aim was to make complex equipment and machinery safer and more efficient. Human factor includes the evaluation of a human's physical and mental capabilities and limitations. The field also helps to understand human behavior during normal and extreme situations. The insights aim to minimize human error. The human factors discipline includes the methods (and became the new term) to talk about ergonomics.

In the aeronautics sector, as well as in Patient safety, human errors are still a significant research field. Human factor research is still used to limit the risks, knowing that in the aeronautics and in the medical sector human errors lead to dramatic failure. Human factor research may help to put in place some strategies to prevent this type of error.

Wars are always a source of innovative technology advancements. Research from the defense sector was then used in the automotive industry and then expanded to other industries such as leisure, sports, etc. Research can help limit the risk of injuries but also can make a product more comfortable to use, with great functionalities, and improve the interaction between the object and the human (user).

Design

Once a product is comfortable to use and technically is the best it can be, especially for the leisure sector, this is when the designer comes in to play an important role: to make the product more beautiful, or trendier. The design has a commercial impact. A good product needs to be technically excellent, to be comfortable, and to look great.

SPORTS

When a ski equipment company creates a new ski boot to improve a skier's performance, it has to use the latest technology to fit the ski, use the most recent materials to make it light, and make it strong enough to keep the foot in place to protect the athlete from getting injured. Over the years, ski boots have become more and more comfortable, as well as looking great and trendy (Figure 1-2). The same thing happens in many sports such as for running shoes, golf clubs, tennis rackets, etc.

Figure 1-2. *Ski boots first generation versus today*

Further, when we look at the boats that race around the world (Vendée Globe), we can compare the technology, design etc. on the boats that were doing the golden race in the late 1960s to the one today and look at how the Alex Thomson Hugo Boss racing boat is an example how it has evolved over the years.

Human and Computer Interaction

Human and computer interaction (HCI) is an interdisciplinary field that is highly influenced by human factor, ergonomics, and experimental design. It involves computer engineering and psychology.

HCI does not involve physical equipment but is more related to software, computers, and interfaces.

Ergonomics research methods and theories can easily be translated into the design of a system and or device. It is essential to keep in mind that initially users of computers were experts such as mathematicians, engineers, the military, etc. They already had excellent knowledge of how to operate complex devices.

HCI research began in the 1980s and was generally used to evaluate, from a usability perspective, how people interact with software such as office programs, SPSS, etc. (Lazar et al., 2010).

Human and computer interaction was also highly influenced by innovation in lab research. Innovative lab research tended to be experimental, using quantitative research methods that took place in a controlled environment. In the 1980s, human errors in the human and computer research became a major topic.

In the late 1990s, computers were introduced into family homes. They were used not only for professional purposes but also for personal ones. The World Wide Web also brought a new dimension to the use of computers.

The emergence of social media such as Facebook in 2004 completely changed the dynamic of how people interacted with computer software and websites. Web 2.0 refers to the end user becoming a content generator and communicating directly through sites (Paul Graham, 2005). Initiating new perspectives, users became more and more critical.

The entire field of HCI changed as it started to involve more than one human and one computer interacting at the same time. The behavior, connection, emotions, and communication operated simultaneously. Computer science research could not manage to gather all the information about end users. HCI research methods were too limited. They could not answer all the questions about human behavior. Psychological research, medical sciences, engineering, psychology, and social interaction were needed to get a better understanding of users.

We should not forget that computers and software were at first tools for the military and research. Not for the general public, they were built for an experienced cohort and specialized people.

From Usability to User Research

Initially, measuring human interaction with software products tended to be based on performance (Lazar et al., 2014), and usability testing was used to evaluate the effectiveness, efficiency, and satisfaction of a system or software.

Usability is related to functionality, the number of errors, and how many users fail to notice a section of a website. In 2008, in their book measuring the user experience, Tom Tullis and Bill Albertin said, "We think that usability metrics are amazing and business decisions are made based on incorrect assumption, 'gut feeling.' Keeping in mind that usability can only be relevant to a product which is already 'live,' or which is acting as the live product with the same functionalities and data. Measuring the usability with metrics was important as it improved the general user experience of a product."

The primary outcome of usability and quantitative measurements was the time it took a user to do a task such as the following:

- Add a product to a shopping basket

- Add credit card details for the first time

- Sign up for an account

- Request a new password

Usability issues are when something on a website or software is too complicated for the user to use. A test will tell you that there is a problem, but it will not tell you why. Quantification of the errors as well as behavioral and physiological metrics tested with eye tracking and facial expressions all helped to evaluate visual appeal, efficiency, usefulness, and enjoyment.

Human Behaviors and Cognitive Psychology

The early stages of understanding of human behavior surmised that the mind was rational and could be managed by controlled thoughts and mental discipline; this is called *rationalism* (Hayes, 1998).

A lot of time was spent conducting experimental design to understand people's behavior. The neurologist Sigmund Freud (1956–1939) took a completely different approach of using dialogue between the patient and the analyst to understand his patient's behavior.

His vision was to represent the human mind figuratively as an iceberg, claiming that most behaviors were unconscious and not rational. Psychoanalysis was used to understand people's problems, especially after World War I, as traditional experimental psychology rationalism could not explain the dramatic outcome of the first war.

With the evolution of new technology during World War II, psychologists (even those who believed in behavioral approaches and theories) realized their limitations and couldn't explain why the computer was not making mistakes when the human brain/mind did.

Psychologists started realizing the complexity of the human brain and continued experimental laboratory research, which led to comparative studies between the human mind and computers. Researchers wanted to understand the mental process, and a new field of cognitive research psychology started to develop. Cognitive psychology uses experimental research to understand and draw an account of the mental process. Empirical research in the area of perception, attention, memory, language, thinking, and perception was booming.

The context in which humans were interacting was almost irrelevant to the researchers. Their primary interest was to identify processes, aiming to create cognitive processes that put all humans in boxes. Unfortunately, any human who did not fit a box was considered as having abnormal behavior or being cognitively impaired.

Social Interaction and Psychological Research

In the 1950s and 1960s, a lot of work in the domain of social and psychological sciences was done using experimental controlled experiments, which used quantitative research methods. At the same time, other researchers thought that experimental research was too limited and missed the reality of the world. They started to create new methods to collect data. Bales developed the System of Human Interaction, which used categorization. Others started observing daily activities of children (Rush & Bateson, 1950). Also in the 1950s, sociologist Evering Goffman (1922–1982) was writing his PhD. He was using observational methods and developing his method of face-to-face interaction, while Harold Garfinkel (2017–2011) was developing and teaching ethnomethodology (which uses common conversation as data) at UCLA.

Social Interaction in Everyday Life

In the 1960s, sociologist and anthropologist Harvey Sachs (1935–1975) was working on his PhD under Goffman's supervision (Figure 1-3). Sachs was interested in how socialization occurs in everyday conversation and developed conversation analysis with Gail Jefferson (1938-2008) and Emmanuel Schegloff (1937–).

Figure 1-3. *Emanuel Schegloff and Harvey Sachs, founders of conversation analysis*

Conversation analysis is based on the audio recording of natural conversation (a help line), and it identifies systematic patterns that occur in everyday interaction.

Objects Involved in Everyday Life

In everyday interaction, we as human beings use objects and surroundings to communicate (Savarit, 2007). In early 2000, a fascinating piece of research from the semiotician Charles Goodwin (1943–2018) investigated people in their workplace (Figure 1-4).

Figure 1-4. *Semiotician Charles Goodwin, distinguished research professor in social interaction*

Goodwin investigated how oceanographers interacted with each other in their work environment and how their work tools in association with gesture, eye gaze, etc., were essential to communicate. Oceanographers were using their computer screens, as well as their communication, to do their jobs. Charles Goodwin's work took a completely different dimension, using eye gaze, gestures such as pointing and nodding, and conversation analysis and discourse analysis. The object (the computer screen) took a central role in the interaction between the different oceanographers on the ship (Goodwin, 2002).

His work influenced social interaction research such as pilot interaction in the cockpit and medical interaction in the operating theater.

There is now clear evidence that objects and digital products play an important role in social interaction.

Collecting Data in Natural Environments and Analyzing It

The most important part of this research is, in my opinion, not only the fact that they used data from a natural environment but that new research methods from sociology, anthropology, and social interaction emerged such as ethnomethodology, discourse analysis, conversation analysis, etc.

They used new ways of collecting data such as note taking, pictures, audio recordings, and video recordings of the interactions in a natural environment. Why video recording? Video recording enabled them to go back to the data any time they wanted. The audio and video data were transcribed, and then the transcript permitted the analysis. Those researchers were looking at the qualitative data and identified systematic practices across the data and participants.

Why use recordings? Your brain can't remember and replay interaction without omitting or transforming the content.

Those methods of collecting data in a natural environment are highly relevant to the use of digital product/service in everyday life.

In the 1960s, collecting data in a natural environment, capturing the reality of the participant, having recordings of data, and going back to them to identify systematicity were disruptive techniques. We can see now how social interaction in everyday life influences the way how qualitative user research can be done.

A Closer Look at User Research

Now that user research has been defined and put into historical perspective, let's take a closer look at its relevance in the workplace. In many organizations, the user researcher has to fight to make sure stakeholders understand that we use evidence to understand who the users are and how they will behave. User research will use different research methods to produce evidence that answers their research questions. We have various tools at our disposal to collect and analyze data. In this section, I begin to give some information about the different research approaches.

While doing research, we have the choice of taking a quantitative approach or a qualitative one. Often, stakeholders prefer numbers to case studies.

They sometimes say to me that numbers provide stronger evidence. I will challenge the robustness of a survey with 200 participants. On the other hand, I find interviews with 20 participants will give stronger evidence. I will elaborate on this research debate in Chapters 6 and 7.

Both approaches have their advantages and disadvantages. They have different purposes and will answer different research questions. The sample size will be different; they will gather a different type of data. When the research is properly done, both approaches are reliable and robust.

Quantitative Research Method

Quantitative research takes a top-down approach, starting with the big picture and using deductive reasoning (Figure 1-5).

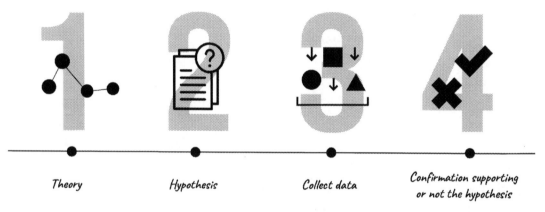

| Theory | Hypothesis | Collect data | Confirmation supporting or not the hypothesis |

Figure 1-5. *Quantitative research: top-down approach*

HOW MANY?

You want to find out how many people visited your website last month. You will take a quantitative approach. You want to find out how many people completed a transaction on your e-commerce site.

Or as part of your digital transformation, you want to evaluate which telephony system your staff is using. If you have 6,000 employees, you can determine how many used mobile phone, landline, and video conferencing systems (such as Skype, Zoom, WebEx etc.). You can do this by creating a survey that you will send to all 6,000 employees.

If you want to validate some idea or a hypothesis, you will also tend to use a quantitative approach.

Quantitative research methods require a large sample; they involve a large amount of data and are associated with experimental research, analytics, survey, etc. A quantitative approach validates a hypothesis, theory, or preconceived idea.

Before starting any research project, I will gather the information that is already there if the digital product is live. I will get the analytics to identify the activity, the traffic, how every section of the website is doing, etc. Quantitative research will answer the questions how many, how often, and when.

A quantitative approach may validate only what is already there, or preconceived ideas. But you will have a large amount of data, and this will have some statistical validity.

On the other hand, you will not be able to answer why or how people are using the website.

You may realize that there is no traffic in one section of your site or that people log into your website to start the process of making a purchase but are not completing the purchase. How do you plan to find out why they did not complete the action?

Qualitative Research Methods

In contrast to quantitative research, qualitative research takes a bottom-up approach (Figure 1-6). It starts from a specific observation and goes to a generalization and informs theory.

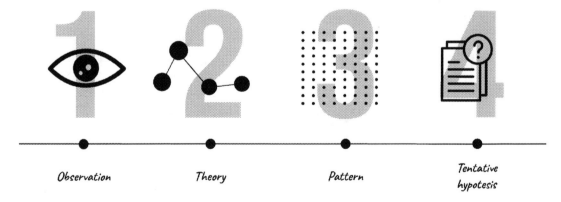

Figure 1-6. *Qualitative research: bottom-up approach*

Generally, qualitative research requires fewer participants (case studies, observations, interviews, etc.) Qualitative approach necessitates an in-depth investigation. Qualitative research identifies phenomenon, common patterns, and systematic occurrence.

WHY?

You have a new product on your website, and you identify through some market research that your customers would be interested in this new product. This new product is available, but after several months you get the analytics, and you see that the sales are not increasing. You want to find out why.

The only way you will find out is to spend time with the end users/clients and see why they did not buy your new product. You may realize by speaking with them that there is something wrong with your site, the process, etc.

Qualitative research methods require smaller samples. The data could be contained in notes, audio recordings, video, or screen captures. It could be observation/contextual inquiries, user testing, interviews, or focus groups.

Qualitative approaches are useful to answer the questions how and why. Qualitative research methods will enable you to identify the reality of the world and see people in certain situations, in their natural environment, showing how they use the product at home, etc.

Both approaches are complementary to create a successful product or service. They simply are used at different times and with different purposes. User research uses quantitative and qualitative research methods.

The Role of a User Researcher and How to Become One

I remember ten years ago when I was saying that I was "just" a user researcher and designing was not part of my skills. Recruiters would say, "You will never find any job; you have to design first," or they would say, "Coming from academia, you are not hands-on."

Today recruiters, whether they are from a big organization or a small recruitment agency, keep asking me when I will be available to work on a new project. Today the market is desperately in need of user researchers with strong research backgrounds.

So, what is the role of user research? What are the differences between user researchers, UX consultants, and UX designers? Which tasks and competencies should a user researcher have, depending on their level of seniority? I will also touch on the debate between academically educated user researchers and the ones who learn on the job. Finally, I will give some advice on how to become a user researcher.

Why Do You Need a User Researcher?

Companies and organizations realized that IT products were not very sexy, and they were not always easy to use. Those organizations decided to spend some money on cosmetics and started hiring and building design teams that could concentrate on beautiful design.

Today many realized that design (even if the profession has now some specialties such as visual design, interaction design, or content design) on its own is not enough to create a successful online product or service.

A produce may look great, but if the user can't use it, all the money that you have spent on your design agency or designers may have been a bit of a waste.

An important point that I keep saying is that users should be at the center of the product design, even if stakeholders, salespeople, case workers, etc., think that they know their users/clients/customers. They may see some aspect of their clients, but how can they anticipate their behaviors knowing that every human has preconceived ideas and their brains filter information based on their own experiences?

If you have never used a tablet or wearable device, or even a computer, how would you expect to know how specific types of users (young, old, business, craft workers, etc.) will interact and react to it?

What happens most of the time is that people, based on their understanding and without any objectivity, will make recommendations for product design.

User Research Compared to Other UXers

Because of the high demand and shortage of user researchers in many countries, we start getting people with diverse backgrounds calling themselves user researchers. If you go to their LinkedIn profile, you will see how long they have been user researchers.

Today you can see many designers who change their profile on LinkedIn to user researchers. A user researcher is not a designer. The skill sets between a user researcher and a designer are different.

Many UX agencies or tech agencies call their staff UX consultants so that they can do both jobs. Mixing design thinking and user research may be a bit challenging. It is probably an easy way to deal with the lack of user researcher on the market.

Role of User Researchers

A user researcher can use scientific research methods to evaluate how users are interacting with a new concept, an innovative product, or a digital product. They are experts and professionals who will understand and assess the behavior of a user in front of a product.

Being a user researcher requires a specific skill set. A user researcher needs to master research methods, moderate a research session, and know which way to guide a user and when. They need to be able to answer the research questions. They should also have a good understanding of the product development life cycle (see Chapter 2).

Being a user researcher means needing to know which research methods to use to answer the research questions and which tools to use to collect the data.

They may use quantitative research or qualitative research methods to gather their data, and this will depend on which phase/ stage they are at in their study.

They will use real users to get their data.

They will analyze their data by using reliable and valid methods to extract relevant information that will facilitate the development of the product.

They will share their findings/evidence that will guide product owners and managers to make the right decision.

Only then can the designer start using the recommendations and requirements to improve the current prototype or the screens. Once they have tested with real users and everyone is happy, the screens can be refined and given to the developers to be built.

A user researcher is a researcher who will use several research methodologies to identify who the user is and how they interact with your product or service. A user researcher will also have a set of tools that perform the following:

- Conduct desk research

- Prepare interview questions

- Collect and analyze data

- Maintain accurate records of interviews, safeguarding the confidentiality of subjects, as necessary

- Supervise junior researchers working on the research project

- Attend project meetings

- Summarize project results

- Travel to field sites to collect and record data and samples as appropriate to the specific objectives of the study

- Prepare other articles, reports, and presentations

- Develop or assist in the development of interview schedules

- Conduct and record face-to-face and telephone interviews, as well as user testing sessions with participants

- Prepare findings for publication or final report

- Guide project managers to determine whether they need user research

- Plan user research based on the stakeholders of client business requirements

- Choose the relevant research methodologies (quantitative and qualitative)

- Identify participants

- Recruit them or manage the recruitment agency

- Prepare research tools and supporting documents, questionnaires, discussion guides, screeners

- Collect data

- Analyze data

- Extract findings

- Make recommendations and help stakeholders to make a better decision based on the research pieces of evidence

As mentioned in Chapter 1, user research is coming from different disciplines. It is clear that people who have some knowledge of some of those disciplines should have an advantage in becoming a user researcher.

Transferable Skills

We know that there is currently no pool of students graduating college every year with reasonable degrees in user research. There is no degree, apprenticeship, or post-grad training available at the moment. We have to be open-minded and try to find people who have transferable skills.

When I look for a user researcher, I remember the first time I placed an ad to recruit a user researcher; I was looking for someone who came from one of the disciplines that influenced the development of user research.

I started looking for people with anthropology backgrounds because someone with an anthropology background is useful in conducting contextual enquiries, looking at discovery phases, and observing user in natural settings.

I was also looking for people with cognitive psychology backgrounds, as they are good at planning a user testing session, planning research, recruiting participants, etc.

People with ergonomics backgrounds are good at seeing what will be useful for users and how a product is going to fit into their daily life, especially in the workplace. Someone with a psychology background should have an excellent research method toolkit, and they will be able to plan, choose the relevant research methods, and analyze quantitative and qualitative research methods.

Someone with an HCI background will be good at usability, survey, and experimental design to test a new product. I do think it is easier to train and mentor people with a related background than with no research background at all. Becoming a user researcher requires excellent analytical skills, objectivity, patience, and quick thinking. Without being a purist, I do think that mastering research methodologies is important.

Here's some background on the profession of usability professional (UPA). I remember several years ago when I went to a UPA conference in Munich, Germany. There were already two different schools of thoughts: the practitioners' one and the psychologist one (or people with some academic-related field of expertise). Coming from one of them, I may not be 100 percent objective.

We are still experiencing the same issues today. So, many people are calling themselves user researchers despite that they have no formal training. Some went through a quick course and call themselves user researchers.

You may find outstanding user researchers who have learned skills on the job and some very bad user researchers who have more formal backgrounds. There is no recipe on how to become an excellent user researcher. It may require some formal training to understand how to conduct user research, but the hands-on experience is also essential.

Good skill sets for a user researcher include the following:

- Communication

- Attention to detail

- Critical thinking

- Technical skills

- Planning and scheduling

- Interviewing

Training

Today there is no specific training to become a user researcher. You might find a couple of courses related to user research in some UX/design certifications or user-centered design academic programs.

Some independent UX agencies might offer training of one to two days. I think those courses are good enough to get some introduction to user research, but they are far from being sufficient to become a user researcher.

Recommendations

If you want to become a user researcher, try to attend seminars, UX research meetups, and related conferences.

Ask in your organization to shadow some user researchers, and try to follow groups online to get some advice from more senior researchers.

I recommend some training, and certain universities organize master classes in the field of digital anthropology. If you want to do want a degree, I recommend the fields of ergonomics, HCI, social anthropology, and psychology. I find design thinking and product design courses do not have enough research courses.

I generally spend a lot of time mentoring junior staff, and I also recommend to other senior user researchers that they should mentor and train junior staff.

Why Invest in User Research?

We are in the middle of a digital revolution, which involves many transformations. Everything is moving online; every business startup and small and large organizations are going through digital changes, led by the digital giants such as Amazon, Facebook, Google, etc.

Users, clients, customers, citizens, or whatever you want to call them—they want to have access to everything at their fingertips instantly, through their mobile phone, laptop, tablet, watch, TV, etc.

Every industry is affected by this digital transition. Large organizations and many industries are being challenged by the flexibility and reactivity of startups and new organizations. If they do not want to die, they must move online by creating their presence through a website or an app, improving digitally their internal processes. If they do not do it, this will have a fatal impact on the future of their business.

The digital transformation is a transition that affects all organizations, as they have to learn how to manage dematerialization, data management, optimization of processes, online sales, marketing, cost reduction, staff reduction, etc. We know that people do not like change. Moving to digital is challenging, especially for institutions/organizations that have been established for a long time. Every time I land on a new project, I can see the same systematic pattern: "rushing" seems to be the common criteria across all businesses that are going through a digital transition. Rushing to start the development is common practice. There is a lack of expertise, and decisions are made without having a good understanding of the business and user needs.

I can't count the number of times I have encountered the following:

- They want the product to be ready on a specific date, which is generally the following week, or even yesterday.

- The development team wants to start coding before they have all the requirements.

- The design and requirements are ready, but the stakeholders or designers decided on them without taking into consideration user needs.

- The end user has been completely forgotten, or only a small portion of users has been taken into consideration.

- They have no time or no budget for research. They jump straight to the design assuming that designers are also researchers.

The marketing team generally claims that they know their users/client. Here are some facts:

- Creating or building a new product in a hurry will only lead to costing more money.

- Making changes will cost development and efforts that will lead to rework. Rework costs even more. It is better to do the research as early as possible to limit the risks and reduce costs.

- Doing research too late, once the product is developed, will point out issues that you did not anticipate.

- The design may not meet user needs.

Do you know anyone who has spent a lot of money on a new website and is not satisfied with the end product? Or anyone who has commissioned a web design or digital agency and once it was delivered realized the following:

- It didn't work!

- It was not at all what they were expecting.

- They did not get more transactions, etc.

STORY

A few years ago, I was at a networking event organized by a chamber of commerce. I met someone from the financial services sector who told me that they were redesigning their VIP client-facing site.

I was interested to know a bit more about it, and I started asking several questions.

I asked: Who was doing it?

The gentleman told me that they commissioned a design agency.

I said that is great, and I asked another question: What is the core profession of the agency?

He said: IT, development, and they also have a team of designers that will work on the design.

I said: This sound great (almost sure that no researchers were involved in the process).

I questioned again: Do the agencies that you are using have a user researcher?

He said: We have the com/marketing team that knows our clients, as well as what needs to be done for the product.

I asked him again: Do you think your communication or marketing department will know what your VIP customers' needs are?

His answer: Oh, yes! They have all the analytics, and they have been working on the branding. They know what is needed.

A few years later, I met the same person at another networking event.

I ask him how his premiere account website was.

His face changed completely, and he said: It is a nightmare; it does not work properly, and our premiere account customers do not like it. We are trying to fix it, but it is taking so long.

The primary requirement for the statement of work (SOW) was given by the communication/ marketing team, without taking into consideration the voice of the users. I am not surprised that their website does not meet their VIP user needs.

This company spent a lot of money for the site redesign. Almost four years have passed, and the solution is not great. They still have to fix many issues. Keeping in mind that any alteration costs even more money to the business, they migrated their clients to this new site, but it's possible that some of their clients were not satisfied and decided to transfer their account to another bank that has functionality and more intuitive digital tools (mobile app, website, etc.)

I have many examples reporting similar stories. The other day, I went to see a lawyer in his office. I have known him for more than 20 years. During the conversation, he mentioned that his company was redoing their website. I asked the same questions as the previous example. I found out that the person who was making the decisions about the website was a young lawyer who had a lot of ideas and had good digital knowledge in IT.

My main concern is that businesses understand they have to redesign their sites, but they do not know how it should be done and rely entirely on their suppliers. They never talk about the end user.

They rarely ask themselves what the user would like to find on their website. Why are they going to their website in the first place? How often will their clients use it? Which type of information are they looking for?

I have worked with many IT companies over the past ten years. I know what the IT product managers and delivery managers will say: "We can build everything in terms of functionality." They have a statement of work, but I'm not sure it reflects what clients want. I am not even sure their clients know what they want in the first place. Most of the time they have a vague idea or concept.

The other day, I landed on another project, led by an IT company. They were commissioned to create a new intranet for a global organization. The IT team looked at the functionalities, email feeds, chat feeds, meetings, documents, contacts, news, etc. But they had no idea how it should look.

The business had some feedback from a survey about what the user wanted, but nothing more.

The IT team said, "We will train people for the onboarding." Developers, IT, and tech people are just interested in functionalities and features. The design, for them, is irrelevant, and thinking about the user experience is just something coming from another planet.

REDESIGN WITHOUT USER RESEARCH

A few years ago, a car rental company redesigned their website. I was just a customer using their website to book a car. It looked trendy and beautiful, but the user journey was broken. I ended up calling the help line to book a car rental.

In short:

- As a user I was frustrated because I could not book online.

- It took me more time than making a booking over the phone in the first place.

- It increased the number of calls at the support center.

- It increased the waiting time.

- Customer satisfaction was decreased.

- The experience could result in losing clients.

- It increased the cost of the support center.

- It would result in extra cost to fix the new site.

This site looked good but did not do any good for the business.

Differentiating Client Needs from User Needs

Client needs tend to be missing or are considered the same as the business needs (we want to reduce the number of emails, we want to communicate directly on the intranet, we want to be able to make a financial transaction on our site, we want as a business to get X or Y, etc.).

User needs are not what the user wants, and they are not what the business wants or what the business thinks the users want. Businesses have difficulties understanding that user research is not going to provide them with what they want to hear. User research will identify what the user needs to perform a transaction, to complete a task, or to carry out their daily job.

Understand User Needs

Understanding user needs is crucial for any product development. Today every user is expecting to get an intuitive product. Users have these expectations based on their current digital usage and habits.

For example, someone who is always on the move will expect to have apps and responsive sites that they can use on their smartphones. They may already be doing their financial transactions online (banking, currency exchange, PayPal, etc.) This type of user is expecting to do all their transactions on their smartphone, or they will be looking for tools that are easier to use across devices. Different users may have different behaviors and therefore different user needs.

While working on a statement of work, the business, designers, IT, and marketing people are not objective, and they will only recommend or make a requirement that makes sense to them.

They all have different motivations. Someone in marketing wants to attract clients, someone in IT should make sure the product is functional, a designer's job is to make the site pretty and cool, and a UX specialist will create a design based on user needs. A user researcher's job is to carry out research to identify user needs and to evaluate how users will interact with the product and services.

Doing user research will result in the following:

- Clarify business ideas

- Identify the requirements

- Test the concept with real users

- Draw an account of the users by creating the persona

- Make recommendations to the UX designers

- Check with IT what is possible to be done technically

- Test a prototype before development

- Evaluate the functionalities

- Evaluate the architecture and layout of the product

- Evaluate content and terminology

- Evaluate how the users behave and what their needs are

By doing user research, you will understand the users. Who are they? What are their needs? Business concepts and ideas will be evaluated; functionality, design, content, and architecture will be tested before development.

The advantages of user research include the following:

- User research enables you to follow an agile method and improve the product throughout product development.

- Making changes before development is far less expensive than doing it once the product is developed.

- Doing user research will limit the risk of failure. It will increase the chance of success and of meeting user expectations.

- The user researchers are objective and have several research methodologies to capture evidence that will help the business, IT, and the design teams to make the right decision.

- User researchers can intervene when you want to change the design of your site or you want to add functionalities.

CASE STUDY

Several years ago, I started working on a project for a gaming company that offered online gambling. When I started the project, I understood that they wanted to redesign their My Account section, as well as add some functionalities/features.

I started by having a kick-off meeting with the stakeholders to understand what they were aiming for, what the purpose of their My Account section was, and why they wanted to redesign this section. I started to ask them if it was possible to look at the analytics. I wanted to understand the traffic on this section.

I asked for raw data of how many people logged in as well as all the tabs in the My Account section that involved depositing and withdrawing money, betting history, etc.

Once I got the raw data for the last three months, I analyzed it and realized that there was a lack of activity in the withdraw/deposit section. I was quite surprised that for a gambling/gaming company, user/clients must deposit and withdraw money.

I went to see the stakeholder in the financial department to ask what other ways the customer had to deposit or withdraw money apart from the website. The financial department told me that the customer could also deposit and withdraw money by calling the help desk.

I decided to go to the call center and observe the activities of the operators. At the same time, I organized our discussion group with the operators to get an insight of the situation. The discussion group was fundamental because the operators are at the frontline with the customers. I asked them the main reason why customers were calling them. It was clear to them that the main reason why the user was calling the help desk was to replace an expired credit card or debit card to deposit or withdraw money from their accounts.

When I asked the operators why the customers were calling to replace the expired cards, their answer was they couldn't do it themselves: once they have three cards entered, they couldn't remove an expired card themselves. The reason why is to prevent money laundering. Once the three cards were expired, the end user couldn't withdraw or deposit any more money to the account.

Call Allocations

I asked the operators if they had any data recording the call allocations. I associated that data with the data from the last three months and identified that there was a correlation between the lack of activity on the website and the high volume of calls associated with depositing and withdrawing activities.

Listening to the Calls

I also asked if I could listen to some of the calls to have clear examples of the user calling the help desk to add a new card, deposit money, or withdraw money.

Issue

The main issue identified was that users couldn't use the website to replace an expired card.

Workshop

Therefore, I organized a workshop with someone from the legal department, someone from the financial department, a lead developer, and the product owner. The purpose of the workshop was to come up with a solution to facilitate the replacement of an expired card on the website.

We had some legal limitations, due to the prevention of money laundering. After several brainstorming sessions, we came up with a possible solution.

Simultaneously the development team and a designer created a solution. We started testing the prototype with real users by organizing user testing sessions. With the feedback from the end users, we improved the prototype until we were happy enough to send the solution to production.

By doing user research, we identified a massive blocker that contributed to the number of calls to the help desk. Furthermore, the fact that the user couldn't deposit or withdraw money directly to/from their accounts had a financial impact on the business.

User research identified the issue and put in place a strategy to fix it. It led to reduced costs in the call center as well as increased revenue on the website.

Summary

This chapter took you through the different disciplines and fields of research that have influenced user research, starting with the military, moving through human and computer interaction, and finishing a completely new discipline. We looked at the following:

- Defining user research

- The role of user researchers and how to differentiate user researcher from UXers

- The advantages to investing in user research, as well as the consequences of not investing in user research

- The difference between clients and user needs and the importance of identifying user needs to create a great product

CHAPTER 2

Understanding Product Development Phases

In the past, most IT products were built following the waterfall methodology, which is based on requirements. The client provides a statement of work with all the requirements. The IT team will work on the architecture, the development, and the requirement implementation. This approach is not flexible and will limit the number of iterations that can be done. Furthermore, you will have to wait several months before you can see and use the product. Business needs, policies, etc., may change, and by the time your product is released, it may not be relevant or may not meet your business needs anymore. This approach can be costly if you want to make modifications after release.

Developers now tend to use the agile methodology, which is much more flexible. It is generally used to build or develop new software. Agile methods allow developers to make changes throughout the product development cycle. You can get more information regarding the agile process by reading the Agile Manifesto, which was published in 2001.

To create a new digital product, we have to go through the following phases, as illustrated in Figure 2-1:

- Discovery
- Alpha
- Beta
- Private Beta
- Live

© Emmanuelle Savarit 2020
E. Savarit, *Practical User Research*, https://doi.org/10.1007/978-1-4842-5596-4_2

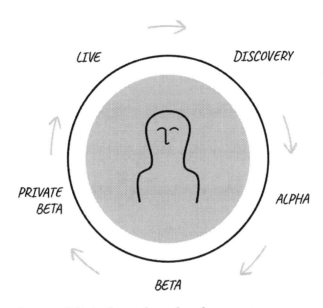

Figure 2-1. *Five phases of digital product development*

It is imperative to go through all these stages. Rushing or skipping any phase may affect the quality of your product/service and its outcome.

In this chapter, we'll review all the phases, including looking at the aim of each of phase, what the composition of the team is, and what to expect for each phase. After that, we will explain how to integrate user research into the product development cycle and which research methods should be used to get the best results to give recommendations to the team.

Discovery

Discovery is the most critical phase; this should happen at the beginning of any new project. This phase generally takes between four to eight weeks depending on the complexity of the project. The aim of discovery is to get a full understanding of the current situation. It helps to decide at the end of this phase whether the project should be moving to alpha.

The team in the discovery phase is quite small and is composed of one or several user researchers, an information architect or a technical specialist (if you have a legacy product), a business analyst (if you have to comply with some legislation), and a product manager/owner (see Figure 2-2).

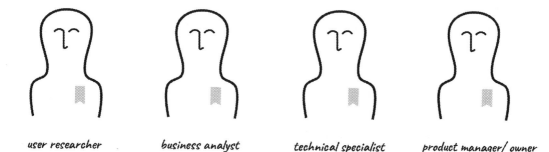

Figure 2-2. *Agile team discovery phase*

During the discovery phase, you will identify the following:

- Who the users are (who will be using the new service)

- What the user needs are

- Which services or products users are currently using

- What is working well with the current services

- What is not working with the existing services

- What the business needs are (why the business wants to get a new service or product)

- Whether there is a gap in the market

- Whether there is a similar product on the market

- Understanding the legislation if applicable

- If there is a need for a new product

The discovery phrase provides a baseline of the current situation and determines whether it's viable to build a new service or product.

The discovery phase requires one or several user researchers. The role of the user researcher in the discovery phase is crucial. Some companies don't see the importance of having a user researcher at this stage and think they have enough knowledge to make the decisions. Nevertheless, the consequences of not having a user researcher may affect the outcome of the discovery phase.

Some stakeholders will make a decision based on their own understanding, which is not always in the best interest of the product. We all have opinions and preferences, but while developing a new product, objectivity is key. The outcome of making decisions without or with little objectivity is risky. The user researcher is a crucial team member; their role is to plan the research, develop research questions, choose the right methodology, identify who the users are, recruit participants, collect data, analyze data, extract findings, and make recommendations based on evidence.

The researcher will identify what the current user journey is and evaluate the pain points, problems, and frustrations of the user while using the service. The user researcher will use quantitative and qualitative research methods during the discovery phase.

The quantitative research methods will answer how often, how many, and how many times the user is using the current service. If it's a new service, the researcher will evaluate how many potential/ prospective users will use the new service.

DETERMINE USAGE

When a company wants to redesign its intranet, it is essential to understand how many staff members are currently using it. How often are they using their current intranet? Which section of the site/intranet are they looking at? Which keywords are they using in the search, etc.?

The qualitative research methods will help to gather data from the end users. Qualitative research is done by conducting face-to-face interviews, contextual inquiries (observation in the user's natural environment), remote interviews, etc. (see Chapter 7). The data will permit you to know how the user is interacting with the current service. If the product is partly online and partly offline, qualitative research will allow you to establish what the user's current journey is and what the user's ideal journey is.

It is imperative to understand the end users. Understanding your users can be done by observing the users interacting with the product. This helps to understand user behavior as well as capture users' motivations while using a product.

By conducting interviews and contextual inquiries, the researcher will be able to identify different types of users. The data from interviews and contextual inquiries will help to create personas, as well as prepare a list of user needs.

It is also necessary at this stage to consider people with low digital skills, and keep in mind that some users may have accessibility requirements such as using assistive technology.

By conducting qualitative research, the researcher will answer these questions: Why are they using the service? How are they using it? What is the current process followed by the user while using the service? Which types of functionality, architecture navigation, design, layout, and look and feel would the user like?

The researcher can also collect information related to the business needs. This can be done by organizing a workshop with stakeholders, conducting interviews, or sending a survey (see Chapter 6). A survey will be valid only if they get enough responses.

Once the researcher has collected enough information, they can draw an account of the user needs and associate them to each persona. After that, the business analyst will be able to prepare the user stories.

EXAMPLE: METHOD DISCOVERY

A contextual inquiry and staff interviews will help you understand how your employees are using your current intranet. Which type of information are they looking for? What is their frustration when using it? What are they looking for in a new intranet service, etc.?

Generally, the product owner or product manager will lead the team, the user researcher will be doing a lot of fieldwork, the information architect will identify legacy products and technical possibilities, and the business analyst will look at business needs as well as legislation constraints.

At the end of the discovery phase, we should have enough evidence to help stakeholders make the decision of whether to move to the alpha phase. Stakeholders may decide to extend the discovery phase to gather more information; if the decision is to go ahead to an alpha, the team can start planning the alpha phase.

Planning the alpha phase at the end of discovery will involve the following:

- Writing user stories

- Deciding the composition of the alpha team

- Identifying possible solutions that will be tested during alpha

- Creating a user research plan

Some organizations such as GDS in the United Kingdom organize a service assessment at the end of discovery, alpha, and beta; you can find the process of service assessment at `https://www.gov.uk/service-manual/service-assessments/how-service-assessments-work`.

A panel of experts (lead assessor, technical assessor and user research assessor, design assessor, analytics assessor) conducts the assessment. The experts will evaluate whether they have enough information to move to alpha, beta, or live. External assessments aim to keep good standards, maintain quality, and be able to make objective decisions.

Sometimes during the discovery phase, we can identify some user needs that were not anticipated. Using qualitative research methods is important at the beginning of a project. Qualitative research methods take a bottom-up approach, which leaves room for unexpected avenues.

UNEXPECTED FINDINGS

When working for a financial services platform and after spending hours on the trading floors, observing traders doing their daily activities, I identified that commodities traders were using their iPhones on the trading floor. Taking a personal telephone on the trading floor is not allowed, but the traders needed to follow the tweets from MEP's (Members of the European Parliament) just before the vote at the European parliament for the Co2 emission cap.

The team came out with an idea of integrating a Twitter feed into the financial platform. This was to meet commodities traders' needs as well as meet the security requirements on the trading floor.

Often, businesses do not find the discovery phase necessary. Often their first argument is because they don't have the budget. Their second argument is that they do not have the time. Their third argument is that they already know their users. On many occasions, I am called in to rescue a project that is close to failing.

The following are common reasons for the failure:

- They didn't take the time to do a discovery; the business or another technical expert created the user stories and user needs based on their assumption instead of using user research to help understand users.

- They didn't have a user researcher on their discovery team. User stories and user needs were also created by the business and a technical expert, not based on evidence research done with the real user.

Frequently, product development fails, because it is led by technology and business needs or because the research is done by someone without research skills. The business or stakeholders decide to build a product/service, without understanding who the real users are, missing the user needs completely as well as the context. If a discovery is made correctly, this will limit the risk of failure and create a clear account of what should be done in alpha.

Alpha

The alpha phase is an interesting part of the process. It is the moment when the team can try different options. We've got an account of the user needs and an understanding of the users from the discovery phase. The team is getting bigger and is composed of the following (Figure 2-3):

- User researcher
- Designer/prototyper
- Content writer
- Business analyst
- Product owner
- Technical specialists

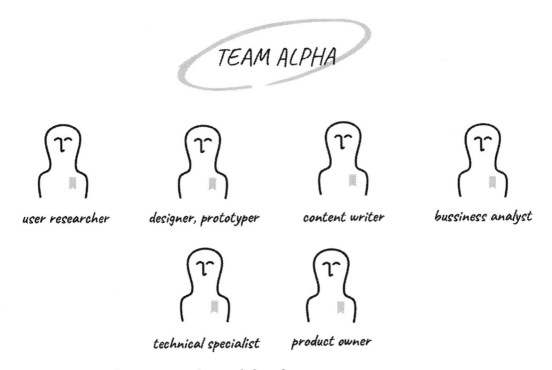

Figure 2-3. *Agile team members: alpha phase*

The agile team should have at this stage a clear idea of the aims of the new product/service. The alpha phase generally lasts between eight and ten weeks for a governmental project; the duration may vary depending on the project and budget. The team at the end of this phase should come out with some possible solutions. They will start creating a basic user journey.

Having a designer at this stage is important. The role of the designer will be to create front-end screens such as sketches, more elaborate on-screen design, or even prototypes. When the new product or service relies heavily on content such as an insurance website, government site, lawyer site, etc., the content designer will also be essential.

The user researcher will recruit participants and organize user testing sessions. Testing all of the screens with real users is essential (real users are *not* internal staff or friends). User testing sessions will enable you to get feedback from users while they are interacting with the new product and also see how they react to a new concept.

The alpha phase can be organized in two-week sprints. This allows the researcher to test different options for each sprint, as well as to keep improving the prototype.

We associate this phase with a trial-and-error process. We create screens; we test them with real users; we get feedback; we check with a technical specialist for a possible solution based on user feedback. The team evaluates whether the solution is viable. If it is, we continue improving the prototype and test it again. On some occasions, you may have some developers who will start working on the backend.

The alpha phase requires collaborative work between the user researcher and the designer to make sure the prototype is ready on time for the user testing sessions. It is crucial for the designer to implement the evidence-based recommendations provided by the researcher.

The relationship between the technical specialist and the researcher is also significant. The researcher will come up with some possible solutions that emerged from the user testing. Nevertheless, it is imperative for the researcher to get advice from the technical specialist to find out whether the recommendations are feasible, to evaluate how much effort will be required, and to see how long it will take.

Important   It is common for a client to have many requirements for a new product. Sometimes the requirements are put into the design first, which can be an excellent way to visualize business requirements. But when it's time to build it, we may realize that there are a lot of constraints such as integration with other services, maintenance costs, or time considerations. In other words, it will be too expensive. It is essential to keep in mind that the agile team is composed of experts. Clients require and expect our advice and expertise. It is our job to guide them and to help them to make the best decision. Many clients or stakeholders do not have a full understanding of the implications of implementing their requirements.

At the end of the alpha phase, the team should have a prototype representing the future service. The prototype should be tested with real users and have been improved after each round of user testing. The user persona should also be updated. The team should have a good idea of what is technically possible and which technology they are planning to use in beta. The team should also anticipate how long it will take to build the new service and how much it will cost to make it. User stories need to be ready to move to beta.

The alpha phase is also important because this is the moment to make technical changes. The design at this stage is to validate the concept. The visual and content design will be improved and refined during the next phase. If the team does not feel comfortable to move to beta, it is always possible at this stage to extend the alpha phase by a couple of sprints. Often there is a rush to move to beta, but it is essential to re-evaluate the solution before moving to beta.

Sometime after completing an alpha phase, the team may realize that you need to revisit your objectives and needs. If new requirements or unexpected outcomes emerge from the alpha phase, this may mean doing another alpha, or even another discovery. It doesn't mean that your alpha is a failure; it just shows that the project requires more research before making a decision.

It is important at this stage to run an assessment that will enable you to make an objective decision regarding the readiness of the project to move to beta.

Beta

The beta phase is a building stage of product development. The team will revisit the findings and the outcome of the alpha phase. They will build the backend and the front end to provide a minimum viable product/service (MVP/MVS). The composition of the team is as follows (see Figure 2-4):

- Developers

- Tester

- Technical expert

- Project manager/product owner

- Designers, prototyper

- User researcher

- Content writer/designer

- Business analyst

- Accessibility specialist

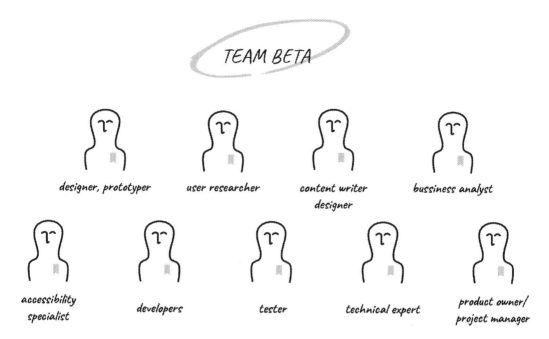

Figure 2-4. *Team members of the beta phase*

It is also essential at this stage to consider accessibility requirements. Many organizations do not yet make accessibility a priority, while other organizations such as the British government and companies such as Barclays already have an accessibility strategy. An accessibility strategy has the objective to make all digital services and products accessible to all types of users. This is also applicable for internal/professional software.

The beta phase lasts between 12 to 16 weeks; again, this is an average because a governmental project duration may vary. The minimum viable product needs to be released at the end of beta. The process in the beta phase involves designing and refining the screens, using a test-improve-test-improve cycle between designer, content designer, and user researcher. The researcher will carry out user testing sessions in every sprint to collect feedback from the users. The Feedback collected will be in relation to the layout, design, content, navigation, and terminology from the user testing sessions. This will help to improve the screens.

The user researcher, designer, and content designer will work ahead of the development team. Generally, the design and research sprint starts while the rest of the team is doing inception (inception is when the team gets ready before starting coding; they review the tools and technology they will be using).

During that time, the designer and the content designer prepare the screen, and the researchers recruit participants and plan the user testing sessions. Ideally, the landing page or the first screen needs to be tested and validated and is ready to be sent to production at the end of the first sprint. The team will start building and creating part of the product; this post-production will be used as testing material. The user researcher will generally request a post-production demo that looks like the build product to use for the user testing sessions with the prototype. See Figure 2-5.

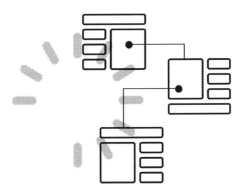

Figure 2-5. *Product in production*

Once we are happy with the screens, the screens can be passed to the development team to build the front end.

USER JOURNEY

A registration user journey for a new service includes the following:

1. Image user journey

2. Landing page (information page)

3. Register

4. Email and password, retype the password

5. Submit

6. Confirmation screen

During the beta phase, the screens created by the designers as well as the content designer should look like the final version. Alteration regarding the color, the content, the terminology, and the layout could be done even after production. It is more complicated to modify the architecture at this stage. This doesn't mean that it is not possible, but making any structural modifications needs to be justified and may involve extra development time; therefore, it will cost more.

The front end should also be tested with people who use assistive technology. This is to make sure the service or the product is accessible.

At the end of the beta phase, the end-to-end minimum viable product should be ready to move to the private beta phase.

Private Beta

Moving to private beta may be a nice way to put live the new service with a small number of users. You can decide which audience you want to integrate into the private beta. This will help you get quick feedback from users in real situations. It will also help to make sure the new service can support the transactions. Private beta is a safe card to play to limit risks and also allow time to make a quick fix before rolling out the product live to the while audience.

The length of private beta may vary; some prefer staying in private beta until most of the features in the backlog are built and released. Others are happy to move to the live phase and release the new features incrementally. Every feature tends to follow the same process: design, user testing, feedback, improve the design, user testing until satisfied, and then send to production.

Live

Before moving to the live phase, we need to make sure that all the recommendations from the discovery, alpha, and beta phases, based on user needs, have been taken into consideration. You also need to make sure that you set up analytics, which are essential to moderate and keep track of the effectiveness of your service. The analytics will also identify the sections of your product or service that are not functioning properly. If you detect a lack of activity, this may be the starting point to conduct further user research to understand why the service has low activity. When the product is live, the team is generally composed of analysts, the maintenance developer, and the user researcher if needed.

Fitting User Research into Your Development Process Cycle

As you can see in the five phases described earlier, the user researcher is involved throughout the product development life cycle. The aim of conducting user research is to understand user needs and how people interact with the digital product. Depending on the phase you are in, the user researcher will have different research methods at their disposal. See Figure 2-6.

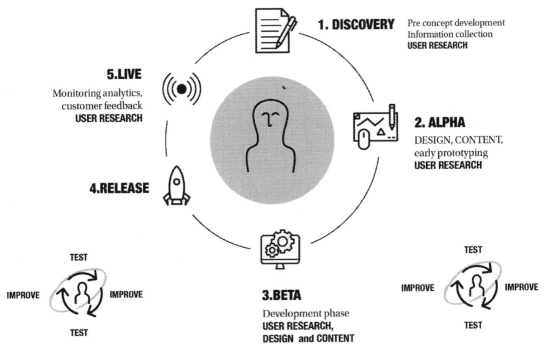

Figure 2-6. *Integration of user research through the product development life cycle*

For instance, during the discovery phase, the user researcher will start by doing some desk research, such as collecting all the information that is available from previous research. Many organizations have a social behavioral research team. They are helpful to provide information regarding the audience. The analytics team may also provide information about the traffic, the activity, and the location of the audience. It is a starting point.

The discovery is also an excellent time to do a competitor review; the competitor review will help evaluate how other businesses with similar offerings are doing. A competitor review will help to understand the strengths and weaknesses of leading competitors. This analysis provides both an offensive and defensive strategic context to identify gaps and highlight opportunities to improve your online offering and understand where you can get ahead of your competition.

The type of review performed is what is known as a *heuristic evaluation* or UX review. This is where a usability expert reviews your website and compares it against accepted best practices and user experience principles.

For this review, we evaluated the efficiency and effectiveness of key user tasks in the following areas:

- Access

- Content and labeling

- Navigation and information architecture

- Layout and brand

- Consistency across the site

- Signup or registration, etc.

Once the desk research is completed, the researcher will identify the gaps and will start developing a research plan accordingly. Once we have identified the audience, we generally organize contextual inquiry, face-to-face interviews, and observations of the user interacting with the current product/service. The aim of this type of research is to get a better understanding of the end users, who they are, what their behaviors are, their motivation, and their needs. The researcher will identify systematic behavior across the participants. This will help the researcher to create the persona, as well as the current user journey.

Sometimes stakeholders who are not very familiar with qualitative research require a larger sample to make a decision. Therefore, the researcher will create the questionnaire based on the findings from the contextual inquiry, interviews, etc., and run a survey to validate the results from the qualitative research.

During alpha, the user researcher will carry out pop-up research, also called *guerrilla research* (see Chapter 7). Pop-up research is quick user testing sessions in which you test screens and prototypes with real users in their natural environment.

TESTING IN REAL ENVIRONMENT

If you plan to redesign an intranet, the end users will be employees. The best way to identify how they are currently using the intranet and which information or functionalities they are using in their daily job is to observe them at their desks.

When we are looking at an app that surveyors are using to conduct a survey to report water damages, it would be more relevant for the researcher to accompany the participant and observe them using the app in a real situation.

During alpha, you can also create the survey to validate the findings from the pop-up research. The difficulty, again, is to get enough responses. The other day, we were assessing a project in which they had done a survey. They sent the survey to 4,000 users. Unfortunately, they got only 49 respondents. The low response rate makes the survey invalid. On another occasion, we got a response rate close to 1,000 respondents, which is very good. During the alpha phase, the researcher can also do card sorting, first-click studies, etc. (see Chapter 6).

During this phase, the researcher will refine the persona and create a clear account of the user behavior, motivation, and needs.

The beta phase is when the user researcher tests part of the production product as well as a prototype. The user testing will concentrate on functionality, layout, content, user journey, terminology, design, etc. The researcher has a choice to continue doing pop-up research or do lab user testing. It depends on the type of users, their availability, their location, the context in which they will be using the service, etc. We can also do remote user testing by using software that shares the screen and records the interaction remotely.

At the end of beta, the researcher must have tested the end-to-end user journey. After every user testing session, I recommend using the system usability scale (SUS), covered in Chapter 6.

Once the product or service is live, the user researcher will frequently request analytics to monitor the activity and effectiveness of the website or product or hardware. If any unexpected events arise, the user researcher can start a discovery to understand why. This will take you back to the beginning of the product life cycle. See Figure 2-7.

Methods

Figure 2-7. *Methods used in user research*

Summary

This chapter introduces how a user researcher is integrated into the agile development phases.

- Agile methods include the discovery, alpha, beta, private beta, and live phases to allow developers to make changes throughout the product development.

- User research plays an important part in the product development by being involved from discovery all the way to live.

- Allocating time for user research is crucial to understand users and their needs.

- Products need to be put in front of users throughout the different phases.

- User feedback as well as the analysis and recommendation from user research helps to improve the product throughout the development of it.

CHAPTER 3

Fitting User Research into Your Organization

More and more organizations require user researchers now. There is currently a high demand in the United Kingdom, in the United States, and in other parts of the globe. You can do a search for "user research" on Google or another search engine, and you will see some interesting results. Online recruitment agencies such as Reeds, Indeed, and even the Jobs section on LinkedIn have many offers.

Some organizations opt to hire permanent staff, while others use contractors. Previously, companies relied heavily on agencies to get their user research done. Now, with the democratization of using the agile methodology to develop digital products rather than the waterfall approach, it is essential to embed user researchers into the scrum team and have them co-located. This is probably why companies tend to recruit people to work on-site.

It is not always easy to find the best solution for your organization to integrate user research. Instinctively, we would think that the integration of user research would depend on the organization's size. However, after working with and in several small to large organizations, both in the private and public sectors, I realized that introducing user research is not that straightforward.

Different types of organizations will have different needs. For instance, a startup may need some user research at the beginning, so they need to do a discovery, but most of the time, they don't have the budget for this. Large organizations such as government departments will require user research regularly and need to integrate user research into their scrum team on a regular basis, as it is mandatory for them to pass their Government Digital Service (GDS) assessment in the United Kingdom (see the description in Chapter 2), while other organizations do not have any idea what user research is and rely on market research to get an understanding of their customers. How you integrate user research into your business will depend on the maturity of your organization.

© Emmanuelle Savarit 2020
E. Savarit, *Practical User Research*, https://doi.org/10.1007/978-1-4842-5596-4_3

In this chapter, we will discuss whether there is a necessity for a business to fail before it starts thinking about user research. I will also explain the different stages of maturity, as well as answer some pragmatic questions related to structuring your user research capability. Finally, we will look at several examples of user research in different case studies, and I will give you some possible solutions for integrating user research successfully.

Do Organizations Need to Fail to Start Thinking About User Research?

For the past ten years, I have observed companies developing products based on technology and design without questioning who the end users were, what the users' needs were, etc. They tended to dismiss user research or do their own research, conducted by developers, business analyst, or designers. They knew that their objectivity toward the user experience may be biased, due to their implication in the project, as well as their lack of research methods knowledge.

When I start talking about user research, stakeholders roll their eyes and say, "We know our customers" or "Our customers will love this new product. It looks beautiful, and they will be using it in no time." They may have a bit of a Steve Jobs syndrome, thinking that the users will adapt to their product and that they are as talented as Steve Jobs. Mozart was a genius, but that does not mean all the young musical prodigies will be like Mozart. I would say the same thing about new technologies and new design concepts: everyone can be talented, but there will always be only one Steve Jobs.

From a user research perspective, developing a new product without spending any time with real users is a hazardous business! Large organizations with a lot of cash may be able to adjust their trajectory if the sales go down or don't meet their expected projection. For small to medium enterprises (SMEs), this is an entirely different story. The result may be dramatic, leading them to close their business or make huge sacrifices to keep the business going. While for a startup, the solution is generally more drastic as 50 percent of small businesses/startups fail in the first four years (Matt Sweetwood, 2018). The reasons are no market need (42 percent), they run out of cash (29 percent), and poor product (17 percent). Not doing any user research may also stop them from getting some funding.

Failing is what happens when an organization starts building a new product without taking into consideration user needs and without incorporating user research into its product development (Figure 3-1). In the early 2000s, Samsung developed some amazing TVs (from a technology point of view). Once the TVs were on the market, Samsung realized that prospective clients were not excited about the new TV. This resulted in lack of sales.

Figure 3-1. *Using internal staff instead of real users*

Samsung decided to talk to end users and set up more than 300 interviews. Once the interviews were analyzed, Samsung realized that TV was not perceived as a piece of electronics, but as a furniture. This insight completely changed Samsung's strategy of product development. Not only did the product need to be high tech, but it also needed to fit a customer's environment/habitat. This user research made the stakeholders understand the importance of taking into consideration the people who would be using their TV, as well as differentiating types of users (through personas; see Chapter 6), which is different than profiling users from a marketing point of view. People's homes are all very different, and people will have different needs, motivation, and behaviors toward a new piece of electronics. Samsung failed to realize the benefits of user research as a way to reduce risks and increase desirability.

This was a clear example showing that failing was the trigger that helped to integrate user research into a product development life cycle. Luckily enough for Samsung, it could afford to fail and to invest a large amount of cash into an emergency user research project. I am not quite sure an SME would be able to afford it. Even if it could, the consequences would be dire. Many SMEs do not only need to go through a digital transformation that is already scary and costly, but user research may not be their top priority. Most SMEs would instead invest in something pretty, rather than understanding the needs of their users. Like another organization that does not know about user research, they can't see the ROI of doing user research.

Some organizations may be aware of what user research is, but they do not believe or trust the outcome. One of the reasons may be that they did do some user research, conducted by a member of their staff or by a designer. People who are conducting user research without any research background or expertise may provide the wrong results that may not impress their client. I tend to say that the client's user research perception and understanding may have been sabotaged. It is hard to get them on board after such an experience. Others have never had the chance of experiencing user research done by a properly trained user researcher. They don't know what user research is, and they will only rely on what other members of their team tell them.

Also, many people generally associate user research with usability. As mentioned in Chapter 1, user research is far more than usability. One of the roles of user research is to challenge the design, the business strategy, the user journey, and the functionalities that do not meet user needs. People do not like to be challenged, but one thing is sure, the role of the user researcher is to provide evidence-based findings using quantitative and qualitative research methods.

Startups have different issues in terms of seeing the advantages of integrating user research. Startups, especially the tech ones, seem to be familiar with UX and digital products, and they understand that people will be using their products. They are much more open to the fact that users are significant. Generally speaking, startups have a better understanding of what user research is. One of the issues for startups is the lack of budget, especially at the beginning. It is common for entrepreneurs to start working on their project in the evening at their kitchen table while working on another job to pay the bills. Even after they have grown a bit, started hiring some staff, and managed to get some funding through friends, family, and crowdfunding, cash is still an issue. They seem to have other priorities such as design first, making something pretty to attract users.

I have identified similarities across startups, SMEs, large multinationals, and the public sector. It is a question of readiness. We all know that business at the moment is in the middle of a digital transition; this does not mean companies are ready for it!

The main obstacle to introducing user research into product development is the maturity of the business. Budget is important, but the main blocker is the lack of maturity, not from a business perspective but related to UX, user-centered design, and user research.

I have been observing client organizations and wondering why some businesses welcome user research while others have completely dismissed the benefits of integrating user research, with the same overconfidence that they know it all.

The following are the different comments that may cause this lack of understanding about user research:

- They already know what users want.

- User research is expensive, and they can't see the direct ROI.

- They don't trust user research because it relies on a lot of qualitative data. They want numbers.

- Many user researchers aren't trained as researchers and may provide the wrong recommendations.

- They don't understand what user research is.

- They think user research equals usability testing.

- Designers do not like to be challenged by user feedback; who does?

- Stakeholders' ideas may be dismissed with user research findings.

- A bad decision could be identified.

- It costs too much money. (When you build a house, will you save money on the research pre-construction?)

It makes sense for you to work with an ergonomist to create a building for people with handicaps. It is the same with the digital product: it is essential to be user-centered.

Sometimes you need to have one member of the leadership team who knows about user research, has worked with user researchers, or has read a lot about it. Their understanding makes the whole difference.

Without really understanding user research, the role of a user researcher, and its benefits, it may be hard for an organization to make the first move. As I said, it is a question of maturity. I will cover the different maturity phases and give you some examples of what you can do to help your organization move toward the full maturity of integrating user research.

What Is Maturity?

Let me take you back to children's development and psychological maturity, which is a helpful analogy. We all went through the different phases of child development; therefore, I will use that definition of maturity as a starting point. Wechsler (1950) is well-known for his intelligence battery test to evaluate children's intellectual maturity.

Maturity is not an either/or quality or a default. It is something that children, teenagers, and adults acquire over time. We talk about neuronal maturity and capabilities, as well as learning new skills and developing the ability to interact with the complexities of life.

This can apply to relationships, intellectual capability, language development, etc. This is part of the life cycle. Reaching maturity is also part of the business life cycle in which a business may launch (startup), grow, adapt to external changes such as financial crisis, go through a digital transition, adopt a new policy, etc., until it reaches maturity, and eventually declines, like the human life cycle.

Business Maturity Phases

Business organizations also go through development phases throughout their life cycle, as well as through permanent changes. Businesses have to adapt and sometimes rely heavily on consulting companies to help them when they have to go through changes, restructuring, fusions/acquisitions, optimization of processes, budget cuts, revolutions, maturity phases, etc.

Paul G. Leslie (2010), in his white paper, described business maturity phases. He associates the changes in terms of leadership through all the stages; this is an interesting read. A business organization develops and grows through a life cycle of constant change (Figure 3-2).

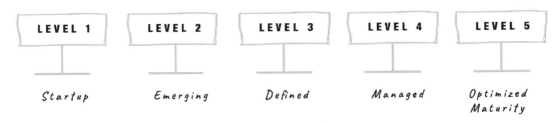

Figure 3-2. *Business maturity model*

Here are the business phases:

- **Level 1:** Startup

  - Passion and excitement

  - Low revenues

  - Planning

  - Fast-paced activities that can sometimes be chaotic

  - Simple processes

  - Multiple roles

  - Super flexible

  - Multifunctional roles

- **Level 2:** Emerging

  - Growth stage

  - Fast expansion

  - Increased revenue

  - New infrastructures (IT, space, etc.)

  - Processes

  - Multifunctional roles

- **Level 3:** Defined

  - Starts to have its space in the market

  - Increases revenues

  - Strategy for long-term growth

  - Start to implement corporate processes

- **Level 4:** Managed

  - Performance management

  - Processes

  - Predictability

- Leadership
- Several business units
- Corporate culture
- Work on retention workforce
- **Level 5:** Optimized-maturity
  - Optimized structure
  - Organizational competency
  - Revenues greater than $500,000
  - Executive team
  - Strategizing growth

Design Maturity Phases

Figure 3-3 and the following list show some interesting components of the different stages of design maturity. They are organized into five stages.

Matt Corrall design maturity stages

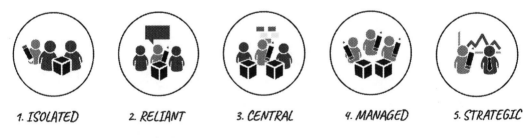

1. ISOLATED   2. RELIANT   3. CENTRAL   4. MANAGED   5. STRATEGIC

Figure 3-3. *Matt Corrall design maturity stages*

- **Stage 1:** Isolated
  - Strategy set by management
  - Scope set by product owner
  - Developers driven by features

- No cross-collaboration

- Second guessing users

- Little or no design budget

- Minor usability/visual tweaks

- Design joint later in project

- Sprinkling of magic

- Culture resistance

- **Stage 2:** Reliant

  - Budget allocated for design

  - Interactive design and testing

  - Ethnographic research begins

  - Some direct customers contacts

  - Research driving features

  - Design "as user expert" in room

  - Work across product teams

  - Minimum knowledge sharing

  - Deliverable becomes lean

  - Cultural barriers coming down

- **Stage 3:** Central

  - Specialism on design team

  - Design on project the norm

  - Product discovery/agile process

  - Design planned and budgeted for

  - Product scoped with owners

  - Regular research and testing

  - Developers using user stories

- User testing accumulating data

- Awareness of design outside team

- Design team spread thin

- **Stage 4:** Managed

  - Company-wide, central resource

  - Multiple digital touchpoints

  - Responsible for experience

  - Scope project to fit strategy

  - Generalist manager picking projects

  - Several specialist design staff

  - Standard usability testing metrics

  - Harmonized product details

  - Coaching of other teams begins

  - Testing evidence of success

- **Stage 5:** Strategic

  - User-driven organization

  - Set strategy with senior staff

  - Comprehensive user database

  - Team road map, plan portfolio

  - Teams have performance targets

  - Work across digital devices

  - Team sets and governs standards

  - Established process company-wide

  - Engagement at senior level

  - Research and test new hypothesis

There are so many UX maturity models, and its definition is not crystal clear. A large organization will start to go through a design maturity transformation, followed by a UX one. UX maturity seems to be the new topic that's *en vogue*. Everyone in the field of UX is coming with their own definition and offering between four to eight phases. However, the issues with UX maturity models are that they are a bit vague, in terms of who is doing what. UX means user experience and may involve multidisciplinary teams, which includes a designer, interaction designer, service designer, content designer, and user researcher (who are sometimes called *UX researchers* or *user design researchers*). In my opinion, the word *designer* is too prominent and may mislead the business, which may end up not having a full understanding of the different professions within the UX world.

I came across the paper "UX Maturity Model" by Lorraine Chapman and Scott Plewes presented at the Human and Computer Interaction International Conference in 2014, which was a good starting point since many people have come up with their definition of maturity models. For example, Nielsen Norman Group went with a simplistic description, in four phases, but recently increased it to eight stages; user testing has a six-stage model, while Nicky Anderson uses a five-stage model in her post on Medium.com. Testingtime.com proposes a six-phase maturity model, as shown in Figure 3-4 and described in the following list.

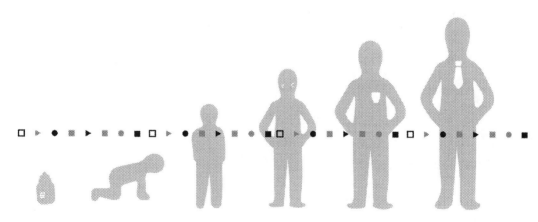

Figure 3-4. *UX maturity model*

- **Stage 1:** Lacking UX awareness. Businesses have no awareness of what UX is, what it involves, and what the added value of UX is. The structure and the architecture are led by developers.

- **Stage 2:** Ad hoc UX. Someone within the organization may have heard of UX and its benefits but without really having a clear understanding of what UX is. There are no allocated UX resources.

- **Stage 3:** Project UX. UX starts to be incorporated into the development process on some occasional projects. They hire temporary resources as they don't have a fixed budget allocated for UX.

- **Stage 4:** Business UX. The organization has systematically incorporated UX into their product development. Projects have to reach UX acceptance to be released. They still need to include a budget for UX in the process, but it is more systematic.

- **Stage 5:** Strategically integrated UX culture. The company integrates UX including prototypes that are tested by user researchers. There is no issue with budget; the main evangelization is to apply user-centric design.

- **Stage 6:** Holistic UX culture. This is the stage in which UX is fully integrated and the business approach embraces a user-centric design, as well as using agile as a process. UX is part of the business strategy.

Nielson Norman Group Model

The Nielson Norman Group model was published in 2006 and talks about corporate UX maturity. Nielson started with four stages and recently increased them to eight. See Figure 3-5 and the following list.

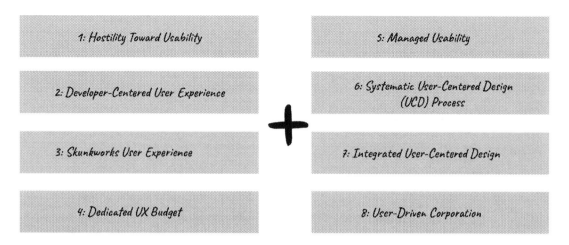

Figure 3-5. *Nielson Norman corporate maturity*

- **Stage 1:** Hostility toward usability. The development team just wants the product to be functional; it has no interest in the users.

- **Stage 2:** Developer-centered user experience. This phase is costly as the team relies on designers or team intuition to create a usable product.

- **Stage 3:** Skunkworks user experience. In this phase, the organization realizes that relying on design team intuition is risky, and the organization starts requesting some data.

- **Stage 4:** Dedicated UX budget. Usability starts to be an important part of the business; some staff on the leadership team understand the importance of UX and have some allocated budget for usability studies.

- **Stage 5:** Managed usability. In this stage, the organization has a UX team, which also has its own manager and budget.

- **Stage 6:** Systematic user-centered design (UCD) process. The company has processes to reach good user experience.

- **Stage 7:** Integrated user-centered design. User research is included from the beginning of the project.

- **Stage 8:** User-driven corporation. In this final stage, the company has a user-centric approach; user research and its methods have a strategic impact.

User Research Maturity Phases

User research may have a separate maturity model with some similarities. Or user research can follow the same process as other maturity models (Figure 3-6).

Savarit User research maturity model

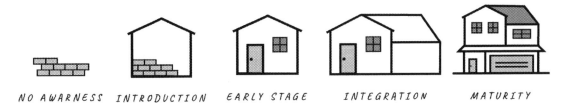

NO AWARNESS   INTRODUCTION   EARLY STAGE   INTEGRATION   MATURITY

Figure 3-6. *Savarit user research maturity model*

The stages are described here.

1. **No awareness:** The company hires a user design agency or designer to make their product pretty and manages to release some budget for design from time to time. The company tends to rely on market research and analytics.

   - **Motivation:** The business is just interested in conversion rate.

   - **Integration:** None.

   - **Team:** There is no user researcher in-house; only sales and marketing interact with users/clients.

2. **Introduction:** The company starts to get an understanding of what user experience is and may get the help of a UX consultant; it may start to get some user testing probably done by the UX consultant or try to do their own research or hire an agency.

- **Understanding:** The business can't really tell the difference between UX and user research.

- **Integration:** There is late-stage testing, but only on limited products; it's experimental.

- **Objectives:** The company has usability testing for live products or for builds before release.

- **Team:** The company may use a UXer, a designer, or a UX agency.

- **Budget:** Some DIY user testing is done by a designer or UXer.

3. **Early stage:** The company starts thinking of having more user research done at an earlier stage and more frequently. It understands the benefit of doing user research. It's not always integrated at discovery but is always present in beta.

   - **Understanding:** The company is able to differentiate user research from design and UX.

   - **Integration** The company tests the beta on a regular basis and involves the team in workshops and observing sessions.

   - **Objectives:** The company understands the users and evaluates the beta and live product.

   - **Team:** The company hires contractors or a permanent user researcher on key products.

   - **Budget:** The company allocates a budget even if it is small.

4. **Integration.** User research is integrated at an early stage of the product development cycle.

   - **Understanding:** There is communication in the organization regarding the benefits of using an evidence-based user research approach.

   - **Integration:** There are small discovery, alpha, beta, and live phases.

   - **Objectives:** The company understands user needs, confirms decisions, and links user needs with business needs.

- **Team:** The company has a mix of permanent user researchers and contractors and is thinking of getting a proper user research capability.

- **Budget:** The company has a dedicated budget integrated into the business plan.

5. **Maturity.** The company starts to see the value of user research not only to reach a great user experience but also at a strategic level.

- **Understanding:** User research is considered as a central and strategic capability in the organization.

- **Integration:** User research is integrated throughout product life cycle of discovery, alpha, beta, and live. There is constant re-evaluation of the product to monitor the product and continue with user research to understand why, how, etc.

- **Objectives:** The company has a clear understanding of who the user is. It does all the following: identify user needs, make sure their product is meeting user needs in relation to the business needs, compare with competitor, improve the general user journey, identify new markets, etc.

- **Team:** The company develops a user research capability, with leads, senior, mid-level, and junior. It starts thinking of having a head/director of user research to manage the capability.

- **Budget:** There is a budget allocation for the user research capability.

Part of the process to reach maturity is to build and grow the user research capability, which is discussed next.

Growing Your User Research Capability

Putting in place, growing, and structuring your user research capability will depend on your organization, maturity, size, and culture. The first thing to evaluate is the degree of user research maturity in your organization.

Create a simple questionnaire to find out the degree of user research maturity (Figure 3-7). You can complete the questionnaire, and once you get the answer, you can have it scored.

User research Maturity Questionnaire

→   **Do you know what user research is?**   yes | no

→   **Do you see the value of doing User research?**   yes | no

→   **Have you done any usability testing?**   yes | no

→   **Do you use any other user research method than user testing?**   yes | no

→   **How often do you carry user research?**

a) Every sprint

b) Every other sprint

c) Only when the product is done

→   **How many user researchers do you have?**

a) Contractors

b) Perm

→   **Do you have a head of or user research director?**

→   **How much budget do you allocate to user research?**

Figure 3-7. *User research maturity questionnaire*

- If the first two responses are no, which is likely when the organization has no awareness of what user research is, you will have to be patient with the organization and make a gentle introduction. (**No awareness**)

- If the third question is yes and the fourth question is no, it shows that the organization has already introduced user research; it probably runs user testing once the product is completed and relies on an agency to conduct the testing. Doing user research is more than checking a box, though. It's about using user research as a strategic process. (**Introduction**)

- If the organization is using multiple research methods but not systematically, this shows that user research has started to be introduced into the product development. (**Early stage**)

- When the organization relies on contractors only, they are in the early stage. (**Early stage**)

- When the organization has both permanent employees and contractors and conducts user research regularly (e.g., every other sprint), they are further along in maturity. (**Integration**)

- When the organization has a head of user research and a predefined budget for user research, it shows that the organization has reached user research maturity. (**Maturity**)

Depending on your maturity and the integration and the growth of your organization, you will look at integrating a user research capability differently.

Research Ops: A New Trend

Kate Towsey introduced the term *research ops* in her workshop #WhatIsResearchOps at a UX conference in Brighton, England. She created the research ops community to set some pillars and support for user researchers. It consists of the following:

- Research environment

- Research scope

- Organizational constraints

- People

- Research admin and logistics

- Asset and knowledge management

- Tools and infrastructure

- Safety and ethics

A research ops function in an organization is there to facilitate a user research capability. Research ops need to be put in place once the organization already has a certain degree of UX maturity and a good understanding of the differences and advantages of conducting research in the product development life cycle. However, I would say that research ops is the tip of the iceberg. Therefore, I will leave this topic to other people who have been working on this.

For more details, I recommend you take a look at the research ops blog `https://researchops.community/about/`, join the research ops Slack, or follow @katetowsey on Twitter to read on the topic (Figure 3-8). There is a lot of information on the Web at the moment.

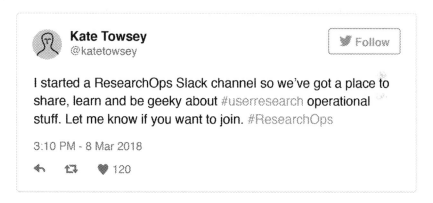

Figure 3-8. *Kate Towsey launch tweet, #ResearchOps Slack*

I prefer to focus on several questions that you may be asking yourself when you are planning to set up a research capability in your organization. I will try to answer those questions based on my own experience. I find that many organizations do not have enough user researchers. The business does not understand the amount of work that doing user research involves. User researchers tend to be overloaded by working across several projects. User researchers are completely stretch and under pressure.

At one workshop I ran on "how to build your user research capability," several attendees said that they were the only user researcher in their organization. They have so many hats. They have to cover all the different job roles, from junior up to head of user research. Every time they asked to hire more people, they were denied.

Finding the right order to put things in place for your user research capability is not easy. Many factors may depend on your budget, the amount of research that you will be required to do, if you have a development team in-house or they are offshore, etc.

Doing User Research: How Do I Start?

Question: I need to do some user research for my product; where do I start?

Answer: Get an agency.

Using an agency to do some user research for you may be the solution, especially if it is a one-off user research project. You may not know precisely what you have to do, and the agency will plan everything for you.

When your organization is in stage 2 of user research maturity, when you want to test your new product before release, or when you realize that after introducing a new product the sales and the traffic on your site is not meeting your expectation, using an agency will remove a lot of pressure. The agency will manage the project for you.

The downside of using an agency is that they will not work with the rest of the agile team. Furthermore, the agency may not have the full understanding of your business and its culture. Using an agency could also be expensive. One thing to keep in mind is that many agencies have UX consultants instead of having user researchers. The UX consultant tends to have a design background rather than a research one. Nevertheless, this could be a starting point. In terms of cost, a user testing project could cost around £10,000 to £15,000 GBP ($13,000 to $19,000 USD); or it could be far more, depending on the amount of participants, their profile, and if you require to hire a lab, etc. (See Chapter 7 for more details.)

Question: I have used an agency several times. I have some annual budget that I allocate to user research. Can I get some contractor to carry the work and be a bit more agile?

Answer: Yes.

Currently in the United Kingdom, many organizations rely on contractors. Contractors are experts who come and go into your organization. They are generally recruited on a project basis, with the help of a recruitment agency or headhunter. They can be onboarded very quickly. It is easy to integrate them into your team; they are autonomous and start to be productive from day one. They can work on short or long projects, in-house or remotely. They are flexible and can adapt quickly to your business circumstances. They are like a staff member but without the long-term commitment. The recruitment process is much faster than for permanent staff. Also, this could be a good way for your business to evaluate if you need a permanent user researcher. Also, in addition to doing the user research, they could help upskill your permanent and junior staff. They cost between £400 and £1000 GBP per day ($525 to $1300 USD) depending on their degree of expertise. They could also be more expensive if an agency is supplying a consultant to work on your team on-site.

Question: We currently have many contractors, and we keep renewing contracts. Is it time to start hiring some permanent staff?

Answer: Yes.

Having a permanent user researcher is a good idea if you realize that you have enough work for them. Furthermore, if you are in the process of integrating user research into your product development, you should consider hiring some permanent staff.

Recruiting a permanent user researcher is a big step. It will also depend on your budget. Can you afford it? Also, know that currently in the United Kingdom it is tough to get full-time user researchers. There are not so many on the market.

Question: Why is there a shortage of user researchers?

Answer: Lack of training.

This is a new profession, and many user researchers prefer contracting over salaried positions, because they excellent daily rates and can benefit from self-employment status or set up their own limited company. There is such a demand in contractors at the moment that it is challenging for companies to afford excellent experienced user researchers. Contractors get a much better deal; it is hard to compete with the daily rate. Table 3-1 lists salaries for a user researcher.

Table 3-1. *User Researcher Salaries*

	Contractors		Employees	
	£	$	£	$
Junior	N/A	N/A	30k-35k	39k-45k
Mid-weight	350/450	450/590	45k-60k	59k-78k
Senior	450/550	590/700	60k-75k	78k-98k
Lead	550/600	700/790	75k-95k	98k-125k
Head	600/700	790/900	95k-120k	125k-155k
Director	+750	+1000	Above 120K	Above 155k

If you decide to hire a permanent user researcher, ideally a senior user researcher will be more efficient and will be autonomous, because they will bring a lot of expertise. Also, the senior/lead user researcher will be able to mentor and upskill junior researchers. They can also identify talent in your organization and upskill them to become user researchers. It is important that a permanent user researcher is supported by the leadership team while building the new user research capability.

Contractor vs. Employee

Some organizations such as British governmental departments rely heavily on contractors; some departments may have around 40 contractors versus 10 to 20 permanent staff members. The lack of equilibrium is an issue and leads to high contractor expense. This is something to work on. While I was the head of research in one of those departments, one of my first jobs was to identify how many employees versus contractors were working in the department. My job was to assess the costs and project how much it would cost to hire permanent staff. It was evident that the department was relying on too many contractors. I created a plan to transition from contracting costs to permanent staff and made a business case to get the budget to hire permanent staff.

I recommend getting some senior contractors and more junior permanent staff. The contractors should be able to upskill and mentor more junior permanent employees. A head researcher may not have the time to do the hands-on work and will concentrate on internal politics when a project requires researchers.

Identifying Talents

As many organizations are going through changes and digital transformation, this is the perfect time to identify talents. What do I mean by talents? They are people already in the organization who have transferable skills with some good foundation or are quick learners.

I find that people who are working on the social/behavioral team, insight team, or market research team have great skill sets that could be transferable. They already have a research foundation, and they know what research is and how to structure a research plan. They understand different research methods. They will learn quickly how to adapt their skills to skills that are more user-centered.

You might also find people who want to become user researchers. People with degrees in psychology, anthropology, social sciences, or ergonomics have good foundations to become user researchers.

In large organizations, it is common to have talented employees who are not used at their full potential and could be a great add-on to the user research capability.

I recommend starting by looking at graduate schemes. (A graduate scheme is when recent graduates get a contract for several years in an organization, which includes a structured training program run by an employer to develop future leaders or experts of their organization.) Graduates can apply straight from university; they start as junior, like a research assistant, and they take one or two years to develop their skills with their mentors.

Recruiting User Researchers

I recommend that you get the help of a recruitment agency/consultant/headhunter. Recruiting a user researcher if you don't know what to look for may be tricky. You can also post the job ad on LinkedIn and another online recruitment site. You will save time if you get an experienced lead user researcher to help you with your job specification. They can also help you identify the right skills for your organization. I have seen people without any knowledge of what user research is being involved in the recruitment process, and they don't know what they are looking for. If you have contractors in the house, they can help you with the interviews.

I have worked in different organizations to put in place their user research capability. Getting an expert to set up the processes, identify internal talent, evangelize user research, and recruit permanent staff, from junior up to head of user research, can also save you time. It takes around six to nine months to set up a small to medium-sized user research capability. The head of user research is always the last recruitment once the team is in place.

Community: Communication Between User Researchers

User researchers are often doing field trips and running around to collect data or analyze it. They are always busy juggling all their tasks. I recommend building a community, even if you have only two user researchers, so that they have time to reflect on their roles and projects and also to talk about their daily work issues, etc. Being a user researcher is exhausting; we are not understood by the rest of the business. Communicating, sharing, and supporting each other is important.

If you have only one user researcher, encourage them to go to user research events and spend time with the user research and UX communities such as UX Crunch, UX Professional Association, Ladies That UX, etc. Having a bit of a budget will also encourage your team to go to evening events and conferences that are great for their personal development, for sharing best practices, and for motivating them. Furthermore, those events are also an excellent opportunity to meet other people, which could be interesting if you are recruiting permanent workers as well as contractors. Those are great place to find suitable candidates.

Leading a User Research Capability

A head or director of user research is a leadership role. We will start to see a growing demand for those roles. Previously, the head or director of UX or design tended to be in charge of the user researcher. Organizations now realize that it is time to get user research leadership in their organization. The role is less hands-on in terms of conducting user testing and doing fieldwork. It is more of a management role, but I recommend that the head/director still have user research skills. The head or director of user research will still be involved in making strategic user research decisions, determining project requirements, managing the resources availabilities, recruiting staff, and helping with research plan, timescale, etc. A head/director of research will be leading the user research community and will also be organizing events for the user researchers to share knowledge, experience, and support each other.

It is also essential to make sure that all the user researchers in the department get the right environment to do their job. It is frequent that user researchers feel isolated and not understood by their peers and managers. They spend a lot of time out of the office conducting field work or locked in a room conducting remote interviews or user testing. They are constantly running after time to complete their work. I have seen on so many occasions user researchers managed by nonuser researchers that end up badly. User researchers do not feel supported and often are looking to move to another job. I recommend that a more senior user researcher manage user researchers. It's difficult when people without prior experience in user research become line managers; this can be difficult when evaluating technical performance, as well as when trying to understand what is the daily workload of a user researcher. User researchers end up not feeling empowered, supported, or understood. User researchers are the ones who should become line managers of more junior researchers so that, at the same time as managing them, they can also mentor and support them.

Furthermore, a pleasant environment is also about having the right tools. It is always a complicated process to make the IT department understand that it is easier to conduct user research with a Mac than with a PC. On a Mac, all the software is integrated, and it does not take half an hour to start the laptop while doing some fieldwork. Even if IT colleagues do not understand why we want a Mac, we all have to go through building a case to use a Mac.

Another point is that it is essential to make sure that user researchers in your organization are supported and aren't allocated too much work. Once when I worked on a project, I was the only researcher for two massive discoveries. I was completely stretched and worked 15 hours per day. This is not sustainable and not fair to the user researcher. It is common that user researchers have too much work, between planning (see Chapter 4), recruiting participants (see Chapter 9), attending all agile meetings, and traveling to collect data. Often user researchers have too much on their plate and do not get support.

While building a user research capability, it is important to set up a nice working environment, offer them training sessions for self-development, and offer them psychological support.

The head of user research will also put in place regular events to evangelize and inform the rest of the department about what it is to be user-centered. The head of user research role provides visibility of what has been done by the user research team; this can be done through show-and-tell lunchtime events or by sending a weekly or monthly blog post of what the team has been doing. Organizing user research surgery is a nice way to support other teams and departments.

The user research leadership role may also take on research ops. This depends on the size of the company, the number of user researchers, and the projects that need to be managed. If the head of user research is too busy to take on research ops, they should get support to help out.

User Research Integration Case Studies

The following case studies are based on different maturity stages.

Startups

It is complicated for a startup to produce a high-quality product with all the required functionalities as a startup tends to concentrate on an MVP, trying to solve a problem in a short period. Startups tend to focus on the design rather than on the research, as they are chasing time.

It is clear that they are in an early stage of their life cycle. They will also be at a different financial stage, which will affect the capacity to integrate user research. Even if most startups have a financial limitation, they also have a separate business maturity. It is like dealing with a teenager; Gloria Suzie Kim calls it "adulting." Startups understand very well the tech aspect, the agile process, and why they should include designers from an early stage. Making their app or new concept visually attractive is also important to pitch for funding.

The issue with startups is not that they do not understand what UX is. I think they are just not ready for it. They are like teenagers or young adults who might have great ideas, but they always think they know best. Everyone else, even experts, who gives them some advice or recommendation is not welcomed. Often startup funders/initiators think that people who try to help them are old and don't understand the new generation or their fantastic new concept/idea. At some point, maybe they are right as most great inventions were not understood at first. Young entrepreneurs have to fight for their ideas and get funding; this is their constant preoccupation. They may find doing user research challenging, as a user researcher makes sure their product is meeting the user needs and that they will be successful. To reach this, we have to collect data, analyze it, and bring evidence to the entrepreneurs that may not always be pleasant to their ears. It is like talking to your 20-year-old son and telling him that he should do things differently, just because we have the experience and the evidence that his trajectory may not be the best one in the long term. It is the same with user researchers; we have the expertise, and our job is to collect data that brings a strong counterpoint to the entrepreneur's beliefs.

I understand that startups do not always have money to pay for user research. There are plenty of students who are looking for a research project for their dissertation or getting some experience. Their professor will supervise them. You could also ask leaders on the market for some advice if they know someone who would be interested in helping a student and mentoring them through a project. Generally, the startups concept is not that complicated as there is no legacy product, and decisions can be made quickly. Any modification on their prototype of built product can be done quickly at this stage.

Before startups go to pitch to get some funding, they could speak to the investor and say this:

> *"We've done some user research. We can see this is working, but it needs some improvement. Also, we have identified some potential opportunities that we did not think of at first. This was the best experience as it helped us to zoom out and see how potentially end users may use our product. We will take the findings and recommendations on board, and we will allocate a regular budget for user research."*

When you say this, investors may not know or understand what user research is, but they will see that the startup is ready to grow up and, therefore, is prepared to move to the next business maturity stage. From my experience, startups that have done a bit of user research made a stronger case for funding and also achieved some maturity by doing some user testing.

Startup Recap

Here are the things to remember:

- Business maturity level 1

- Minimal budget

- Rather spend money on design than in user research

- Do not like to be challenged by a user researcher

- Will probably fail unless some investor or shareholder pushes them to do user research

The next stage, if they have the budget, will be integration.

An Organization That Has a Bit of Budget for User Research

I worked on a project that was an online subscription product (sending products by mail to their clients). The company had a business maturity level of 3 and 4, which means they were generating revenue; they were already well established in the market and just got some investors. They also had a certain maturity regarding the design, since they had a contractor/freelancer who was helping them with their website. It was slick, pretty, trendy, and pleasant to the eye.

Regarding the company's UX maturity, they used a bit of UX jargon without having a full understanding of what it meant. I would put them at stage 2 UX maturity. They were relying heavily on marketing and sales as the primary source of insights for their business strategy. The freelance designer was involved in the decisions, and it was through his recommendation that they decided to call us for some user testing. It was their first experience in getting some user testing and any user research.

They hired us, a small user researcher agency (probably because we were more flexible and were cheaper than a bigger agency). We held a competitor review as well as some user testing, which they called usability testing (see Chapter 7). The marketing team still had a lot of input into the project and may have influenced the progress of the project.

The research provided a lot of evidence-based results.

The user journey was broken: people got frustrated as if they wanted to buy their new product, because they add their credit card details again even if they had already subscribed to one of their products and the company already had their card details.

We also identified that there was room in the market to offer their product in-store instead of relying only on subscription. Many more findings were identified. They had mixed feelings about the user research, as some findings were challenging the design, and the marketing team especially got a bit frightened by the results. They took into consideration some of the findings and disregarded others due to their lack of maturity. Nevertheless, I could see in the next 12 months that they had applied most of the results.

Budget Recap

Led by marketing, sales, and design, these companies do not like to be challenged by user research findings. With a bit of time, they will move to the next phase and probably hire a user researcher on their team or continue hiring contractors or a small agency to do their user research.

An Organization That Needs to Transform But Is Not Mature

I worked on one project in a private-sector company with a lot of old-fashioned institutionalized habits. They seemed to be ready to integrate user research into their new venture of transforming their website to make their institution more appealing to overseas customers.

In terms of business maturity, they were probably at level 4 or 5. They could anticipate some struggle in the next few years to new governmental policies. This would affect their public funding as well as the fee that their customers/users would pay.

In terms of design maturity, they had done some rebranding and had some web designers involved for the last few years. The web team was in-house. Regarding UX maturity, it is difficult to say as they started the project with a content review, which led to creating a business case for a team of 15 content designers and a couple of user researchers. The primary motivation was the reduction and simplification of the content of their website. From a UX perspective, this shows a perfect maturity; nevertheless, no work on information architecture of their site was done, and no interaction designer was involved in the project. After several people mentioned needing an interaction designer a couple of weeks later, they hired a UX designer. They had some delivery/project managers. Two discoveries were put in place with only one user researcher.

The other user researcher was on the beta project, which never had any discovery. The leadership/management team was probably excellent in terms of managing content writing and even had a team of content designers in one building called the "content factory." Regarding the user research, though, management had no idea how to manage user researchers, asking the researcher to deliver and plan the next phase before we got any data from a discovery phase. The researcher was on two projects at the same time, which is not recommended, especially in an agile environment. The maturity regarding user research was between 0 to 1; they seemed to do it to check the box, but not with any motivation based on being user-centered and to make decisions based on proper research findings.

Transformation Recap

Here's what to remember:

- Mature business with cash to allocate to an agile project

- Partial knowledge of UX, better understanding of one of the disciplines within UX, in this case content

- Managed by the wrong people, people without management skills, just focusing on delivering content

- Will start getting some interesting results

- Applying feedback to the alpha phase

- Hard work for the user research (constant battle, lack of resources, more managers than doers, lack of understanding from the management of the time it takes to do the work)

- May fail several times through the process and learn from it

- Use contractor and will probably hire user researchers later

Organization in Progress Surrounded by the Right Expert to Help Them Go Through Maturation

This case study is a large multinational organization with a business maturity of 5 and in design maturity stage 3 or 4. The marketing and communication department was in charge of the digital presence. It was a struggle between the IT department and the marketing department because of a lack of communication. Their UX maturity was at a level 2 or 3 sand their user research maturity was at level 1 and they had the chance to have a CMO who had a good understanding of user testing, eye tracking, etc. It always helps to have someone in leadership with a positive attitude and some knowledge of the profession.

The company hired an IT agency to work on a new project, and they also hired a UX specialist who was also an expert in user research. The company took on board the recommendations from the UX specialist. It integrated user research into its product development, which was a hybrid waterfall-agile process. The results were excellent; after doing discovery and an alpha, they were able to quickly pivot with the support of the user research evidence. They used user research as a strategic input to make their decision.

Expert Recap

Here's a recap:

- Mature business

- Some UX knowledge

- User research integrated by change

- Will now do user research to make their decisions

The Public Sector in the United Kingdom

The public sector in the United Kingdom is a fascinating example. Departments such as GDS, Home Office, DWP, DfE, etc., are mature public-sector organizations and in phase 4 or 5 of the maturity scale for UX and user research. Others like smaller local authorities, boroughs, or government-funded bodies are probably at phase 3 in terms of user research.

The interesting strategy that the United Kingdom took was that every public-facing product/service has to go through an assessment. Specifically, after every phase of product development, every citizen-facing project that involves a certain number of users has to go through an assessment to make sure that it meets the government digital service standards. It is essential to understand that every development of a service has to follow a specific process and standards that include user research. This makes user research integration into the product development process compulsory. All digital projects should be user-centered and follow the GDS principles (see the service manual).

The reason for the assessment is to make sure every governmental product or service follows the same process, pattern, and standards that have been validated by conducting user research.

Putting in place the assessment was fundamental in the integration of user research into the product development through discovery, alpha, beta, and live. The assessors will fail a company that does not conduct proper user research within product development; failing a company is not to punish them but to make sure they think about the users. On so many occasions products are developed from a development and functionality perspective without taking into consideration the end users.

As a user research assessor for GDS, I failed several projects due to a lack of user research or because the team was saying they were conducting user research just to check the box. As an assessor, I generally don't make many friends! I try to be objective and help a team to pass their assessment, but if they are not willing to incorporate user research with the right attitude, there is no reason why they should pass.

This strategy is to force every digital/delivery team (external suppliers, internal team based on expert contractors as well as civil servants) to follow the GDS standards and principles; in my opinion, making every department apply a user-centered approach is the right approach.

Many departments have reached the right level of maturity and now are experiencing other problems/issues, such as recruitment and the decision to hire contractors versus permanent staff. Other challenges are knowing how to manage a user research team, how to support the user researchers, how to standardize the processes, and how to choose which tools they should use across all departments?

Public Sector Recap

There is no magic recipe for setting up a user research capability; the main thing is to try to do your best. It is also a trial-and-error process. You can ask people in the UX and user research communities to give you some advice. Another solution is to hire someone experienced in setting up a user research capability.

Summary

This chapter introduced how user researchers are integrated into different types of organizations depending on their maturity.

- When integrating user research into different types of organizations, the method or strategy may not be the same depending on their user research maturity.

- Depending on the business and UX/user research maturity, the organization may rely on an agency, contractors, or permanent staff.

- Understanding the organization's user research maturity is important before developing the user research capability.

- Understanding the role of a user researcher is essential as well as acknowledging that user researchers are usually stretched, under resourced, and not understood by the rest of the organization.

- Evangelizing user research is a starting point.

- Getting help to recruit your user researchers may be wise.

The next chapter will look at the different issues and questions that a director of user researcher may have. I will use examples and my personal experience.

CHAPTER 4

Preparing for Your Research

Whether you are a product owner, a stakeholder, or a service designer, it is essential to plan your project ahead of time. It is precisely the same with user research. There is a clear step-by-step process to go through before starting research.

The process may vary depending on the stage or the phase you are. I highly recommend you look at whether you require user research at an early stage.

Skipping the discovery phase is common. Once you arrive in alpha, or even close to the beta phase (see Chapter 2), user research ends up being rushed. Ideally, user research should occur at the beginning (see Chapter 2).

You need to find out who the relevant people to speak with are, how to get the budget to conduct your research, why you want to include user research in your project, how to get a researcher, and finally who you need to involve in this project. This chapter will present the steps you should follow before starting your research project (Figure 4-1). Following these steps will save you time and money in the long run.

© Emmanuelle Savarit 2020
E. Savarit, *Practical User Research*, https://doi.org/10.1007/978-1-4842-5596-4_4

Figure 4-1. *Process before starting a user research project*

Before Starting

Before starting to build any new service product or a new feature, it is essential that you ask yourself a few questions:

- What are you trying to build, solve, or sell?

- What is the reason for creating this new service or product?

For example, before creating a new digital service for the government, you have to try to understand why you are creating it; it could be to get rid of paper and create an online application to apply for a visa or a passport or to change your address on your driving license. Here are some other examples:

- You may want to sell a new product and have to create a new section on your current e-commerce site.

- It may be that you already introduced a new product, but the stats do not show any sales.

- You may want to reduce the amount of email your employees get and want to improve collaboration in your organization, so you want to put in place a new intranet that will solve those issues.

- Sometimes you want to replace an existing product or get a new supplier.

In any of these cases, before you start, you need to have a clear account of what you are trying to do, what problem you are solving, and the reason why you want to do it. Once you know all that, put it down in writing with straightforward words.

- Is there any legacy product?

Once you know what you are trying to do, it is essential to find out if your company is currently providing some service already.

Do you have a current online platform? Or a website? Or an agency? Or an existing supplier? Find out what the current situation is so you know if you will need to integrate any software or if you have to build onto something that is already there.

Are you trying to replace a "burning" platform? (This is when the supplier will stop offering a digital product that you use or it is the end of the contract.) Here are some questions to ask:

- What are the implications of getting a new supplier?

- Is it a service? Or is it a product? What is the difference?

- If it is a service, is it a digital service or a nondigital service?

- If it is a product, do you have any competitors?

If it is a new product, you need to evaluate if there are any competitors on the market, what they have done, what they are currently doing right, and what they are currently doing wrong. Are you planning to improve your current product or service? What is the reason for wanting to do it?

Working with Your Team and Getting Support

If you are a product owner, you need to make sure that all of the people working on the project are also involved in deciding to do some user research.

I highly recommend you discuss with a senior person or head of research who can advise you on whether you need some user research. Getting advice at this stage is necessary; the senior or head user researcher can provide you with arguments that will be useful for your business case. If you have an internal user research capability, it should be quite easy for you to access user researchers. But if you don't have any user researchers in-house, it is always possible to contact user researchers through research communities, at UX events, or even through LinkedIn or Twitter.

Some people, such as event contractors, freelancers, or research agencies, are willing to discuss possible projects if you contact them.

I am always available to provide advice to prospective clients or even startups that can't yet afford user research. Also, I can recall several occasions when I gave a lot of advice and even provided research plans in meeting and then later found out that those companies implemented my plan with internal employees, junior, interns, etc. Unfortunately, people who don't have experience will probably take the wrong approach and even provide results that may be wrong. Relying on the recommendations made by nonexpert researchers may lead a project to failure.

Dismissing User Research

User researchers will probably not go in the direction that you expect. The user researcher is there to challenge assumptions, gather evidence, and make a clear account of who the users are, what their needs are, and that the product or services you are trying to build is usable by everyone. On many occasions, I see product owners or other stakeholders not happy with the research results, as it does not support their assumptions. Researchers receive criticism frequently that their results are not welcomed and sometimes dismissed.

DESIGN INTUITION INSTEAD OF USER RESEARCH

Once I was introduced to a financial company specializing in currency exchange. They asked me to plan some user research, and they were very interested in it. I spent several meetings at their office. One day, a lead designer came into the organization and said, "We can fix everything with a new design. We know our clients; we don't need user research." The company took a significant risk to rely only on design, and the user journey is still broken today as the design could not fix all the problems.

In this case, the designer was overconfident, and in my opinion, he took a significant risk by dismissing user research. This was not to save money; it was more to avoid feedback that wasn't supporting the creative idea of the design.

In other cases, the motivation not to involve user research is to save money. User research costs money, it takes time and expertise to plan, and the researcher has to identify the real users, to choose the appropriate methodology, to collect and analyze data, and to extract significant findings that will be translated into actionable recommendations.

By dismissing the importance of conducting proper user research, it shows a lack of respect for the profession. Without realizing it, a company will waste its time by not doing or involving user research correctly. Finally, they will probably spend more money trying to fix problems that could be avoided in the first place if they did proper user research up front.

I understand it is always challenging to find a budget for user research, especially for startups and small businesses, but when large organizations decide to take shortcuts, it will have a boomerang effect.

Do You Need User Research?

From a user research perspective, this is one of the most critical questions to ask. Who are the current users, and who are the prospective users? How old are they, what is their gender, and why will they use the service or the product? Who are they? The first question to ask yourself, is "Does my product/service involve users?" If it does not include end users, you will probably not require any user research. This sounds logical, but some stakeholders want to do user research even if the product does not involve any participants. On the other hand, if your product or service involves some users such as employees, customers, students, citizens, etc., you will likely need to consider doing some user research.

What Do You Already Know?

If you want to save some money and if you have the resources internally, you can start by looking at what is already there. Many organizations have done some research in the past; it could have been in the marketing, social behavior, or analytics department. Reports may be stored somewhere. Any data you have is handy.

If you are in the alpha, beta, or live phase, you should already have some information from the discovery phase. You may realize that no user research has been done in the previous phases, and this is probably the time to start, since you don't have enough knowledge about the users and their needs.

You may have some marketing information about your clients. What do you know about them? What don't you know? Once you have gathered all the available information, you can find out what you don't know; this is the time to identify the gaps and priorities that you want to find out.

Identify the Gaps

Identifying the gaps is the starting point of conducting user research and finding out what you don't know. You may think you know your clients, from a salesperson's perspective, but do you know when the users are using your product? Which devices do they use? It is probably better to identify this sooner rather than later. What is the current user journey? Is there any blocker through the user journey?

At the beginning of every project, it is crucial to identify what you already know. For example, look at previous research, not only from user research but also from data sciences as well as marketing. By reviewing previous research/reports, you will identify what you don't know—identifying the gap to determine what is missing. Identifying a hole in the market means understanding what your product could also offer to the users.

Once I was redesigning a business-to-business portal, which managed the data subscription for a financial platform. As well as redesigning the portal, we looked at changing the business model. At the same time as doing the user testing session, we identified that users (on the client side) were all using specific software. The research permitted allowed us to identify the gap and recommended integrating this software into our portal. This would have a significant impact on the users because it would mean less back and forth and more optimization of their activities. See Figure 4-2.

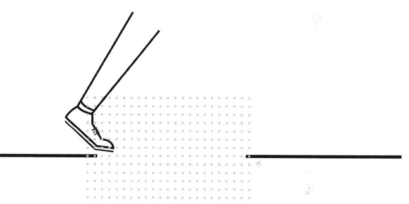

Figure 4-2. *Identifying the gap*

What Do You Want to Find Out?

At every stage of product development, we want to find out certain things, such as the following:

- Who the users are, including the different types of users such as assisted digital and accessibility users

- How they are using the product and service and why

If the product is already live, consider this:

- What is the end-to-end user journey?

- What is the traffic, etc.?

- Do you want to get a better understanding of your product and your competitors?

The user researcher will help you to put in writing all the high-level research questions. If you don't have a user research capability, you can always contact an agency to help you for the pre-project requirements or ask freelancers/contractors to help you refine your research questions. If you have a user research capability, use it.

High-Level Plan or Brief

If you have a user research capability in-house, you should ask the team if they have a template/form that you can complete. The form will help you get a better idea of what you want to do, and it will help the user researcher to evaluate whether you require user research.

I also recommend doing a face-to-face meeting with the head of user research, who will ask you more questions related to the brief; this is for them to get a better understanding of what is needed.

If you don't have user research capability, you can use an agency or request a freelancer/contractor to supply you with a brief (Figure 4-3) and discuss with them what you would like to do.

Brief form

→ Name of the project

→ Phase of the project

→ How many weeks for this phase?

→ What are you trying to solve?

→ Who are the users

→ Is your product and service live?

→ Research question

→ Do you have analytics? yes no

→ Do you have previous research yes no

→ Do you have previous research before for this project? yes no

Figure 4-3. *Sample brief form*

If the brief does not provide enough information, you should organize a workshop with stakeholders to get a better understanding of what they are trying to do for the following reasons:

- To understand the aim of the research project.

- To draft the research questions.

- To understand who the participants/ users are/ will be.

- To find out the time frame. It is always essential to put a deadline on your research. Often when we ask clients when they want the results, their answer is "yesterday."

Build the Case and Present It to Stakeholders

You don't discuss user research in the hallway with your stakeholders. If you want to get a budget, you should have a strong case so the stakeholders can understand the benefits of doing user research, why now, and what the Return On Investment (ROI) is.

If you have already done all the planning, you can prepare a beautiful slideshow, explaining what you are trying to do with your product or service. You can also present some kind of recap of what you already found out with analytics, previous research, etc.

It is always important to find out what the goals of your stakeholders are. These can also be incorporated into your research brief. Considering stakeholders needs in your proposal will help you get them on board.

What do I mean by building a case? You need to make sure that you are not reinventing the wheel. You need to have a clear account of what you are trying to do and why, what the benefits are of doing it, and what the risks are of not doing it. It is essential to include some numbers that will speak to the decision-makers.

Which Resources Do You Need?

Once you have your high-level plan, then you can start thinking about the resources that you may need for your research project. If you have an agile team, I recommend getting user research person to work on your scrum team. It is essential for the user research person to understand the culture of your organization as well as having access to people internally to provide some insights.

A user research agency can be useful if you are using external IT suppliers to build your solution, and they may have enough power and experience to help you communicate with your suppliers.

Note Sometimes your IT or design suppliers say that they also supply user research. Be careful, as they may not have the resources to do this; they will just get a third party to do the user research work. I have come across large agencies/ IT/consulting companies that say they have user researchers, but in reality they hire a contractor who will work on the proposal and do the work for them.

In the end, they are charging you a lot for it, and they take a significant cut, leaving the user researcher/contractor with a lower rate. It may be easier for you to use those agencies that provide you with the resources for your project, but it may be cheaper for you to use a recruiter or headhunter to find you the right person for you at the right price.

You may find some agencies that specialize in user research; make sure that they are not supplying you with a UX consultant instead of a user researcher. Their UX consultants tend to be designers or business analysts instead of user researchers.

If you have some internal capability, it would be easier for you to get some support from them, and they can tell you when they will have a user researcher available. They may also help you with the estimate to see whether you need a lab, specific equipment, and a participant recruitment agency.

Get an Estimate

Do not hesitate to shop around and get several quotes for the project. If you plan to incorporate a user researcher on your agile team, you may ask an agency to supply you with one of their researchers; you can also request a recruiter/headhunter to find you a freelancer/contractor. Many user researchers are contractors, and they are excellent, sometimes much better than the one supplied by big agencies. You can also look at agencies and see what they can offer you for your budget. Some agencies are more expensive than others; it is worth getting several quotes that specify the expertise of the user researcher that they will supply you.

If you do not work agile or do not need someone in-house, you could get an agency that will conduct the user testing, the discovery, etc.

Even if some people tell you that you choose your research methods depending on your budget, I disagree: you need to figure out first what you want to find out based on your research brief; then the researcher will be able to decide which research method will be the more appropriate to answer your questions. Only then can you get a quote or estimate. Not the other way around.

Get Your Budget

Getting your first user research budget is not easy; doing user research is expensive.

It is not always easy to sell user research to your organization. Is this because many companies do not have a good understanding of what user research is? Or is it because they can't see any benefits of doing user research? They are very often confused by UX and user research (see Chapter 1). There is always the question of the budget as well as time restrictions. Evangelization for user research and its benefits is fundamental. If you have a researcher in-house, it may be easier to get someone on board to support you. The main issue that you will experience is having a user researcher available to carry the research for your project. A less successful organization may not have a user researcher in-house and will have to recruit a contractor or to commission an agency to do the work for you. For those, you will have to get some budget. To start this project, you will need to sell user research to your manager and stakeholders. It is always challenging to sell user research, especially if you are not a user researcher.

It is essential to adapt your arguments depending on your audience. For example, if a politician has a great idea, probably supported by political ideology, they may not be pleased to have some user research done. User research may challenge their ideas, which is not welcomed by everybody. But if you say that user research will evaluate the plan and identify how it will affect the end user, provide evidence of what the criticism will be. The evidence can help the politician to adjust his plans, to respond to any criticism, to modify the project, or to even make a U-turn.

```
NEW LEGISLATION
```

Several years ago, one French politician proposed a new tax for French people living abroad. I got so many complaints from the French community in London that I decided to collect data and conduct user research discovery on this matter. I evaluated the impact of this new taxation.

I had many pieces of evidence of the negative impact, including a financial, emotional, and cultural impact on people. The most significant implications for the politician were that presidential election was around the corner. The impact of implementing this new legislation had a direct effect on the votes.

After sending a correspondence to the political leaders with the overview of the results and the consequences of implementing such legislation, they removed the legislative bill. Even though removed, it was probably too late to counter the negative impact. Telling people a story like this helps them to understand what the benefits are of conducting user research.

I recommend starting with a small budget. Some user testing sessions can bring a lot of insights, and you can follow up with a survey with more participants. In some organizations, the budget will come from the marketing or communication department. In other organizations, the IT department will provide some funds. If you are lucky, you may have a UX budget or even a user research lead who will have a budget. You may have some internal sponsor who will support your project and help you by giving you some budget. Startups may struggle to get a budget for user research, but they could do some crowdfunding or get their investors involved.

Recruit a Contractor or Commission an Agency

Once you have your budget, you can start recruiting the relevant solution for your project, whether agency or contractor. Every company is different; some may prefer agencies over contractors. Again, you can get new quotes and contact the people who helped you with your business case.

Statement of Work/Brief

Get your statement of work or brief ready (Figure 4-4), with all the requirements, objectives, deliverables, deadlines, etc.

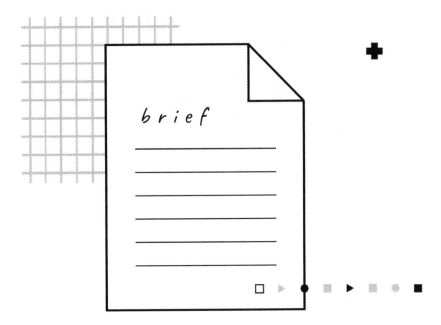

Figure 4-4. *Brief*

Start

Now that you have gone through all the different steps from Figure 4-1, you are ready to start your research project.

Summary

This chapter looked at the process of how to get ready before starting a user research project.

- Identify if you need user research for your product.

- Review the research that was done in the past and identify the gaps.

- Identify your users.

- Build a case to get budget for your project.

- Get your stakeholders on board to support the project.

- Put in place the relevant capability to conduct the research.

CHAPTER 5

Research Preparation

The previous chapter covered how you prepare for a research project and that you need to answer questions regarding the goal, research questions, budget, resources, and statement of work. The researcher is involved in this process, but it is from a product/project management perspective. This chapter is related to the research project preparation that is done by the researcher.

Planning or preparing a research is essential; I have seen many organizations skip this phase. This phase of planning is, in my opinion, the most important step of any research project. Could you imagine any medical, psychological, or social research without any plan or protocol?

Protocols

A protocol is "a document which specifies for a research project the procedures for recruiting participants and gathering and managing data, with which all project staff agree to comply" (BPS, 2014).

I tend to use the phrase *research plan* in a nonacademic environment. I find that in the corporate world, it is essential to adapt the terminology to the field you are working in; also, the word *protocol* may be a bit pompous outside the academic context.

It doesn't matter what you are investigating, which participant you are going to approach, or which methodology you are going to use. Planning your user research is about following a systematic process. You, as a researcher, should follow the same approach every time and go through the same steps all the time. It is also essential to document the research plan, and this document does not have to be too long. I try to prepare a digestible document with the plan, generally one or two pages.

© Emmanuelle Savarit 2020
E. Savarit, *Practical User Research*, https://doi.org/10.1007/978-1-4842-5596-4_5

Why Document?

It is essential to have some description of what you are planning to do. You can share the research plan with your stakeholders and other members of your team. It shows a rigorous process and may help people to understand what the user researcher will be doing. Also, if you share your research plan, you may get some feedback. Sometimes you may have missed some of the questions that the stakeholders want to cover.

Having a research plan will help to have some traceability and prevent the chance of duplicating work.

Record what was done and when, especially if you want to replicate the research to evaluate your service one year or two years later; that way, you can reuse the research plan to replicate the identical study done previously.

If your organization uses contractors, it also helps to have some records and hand-over documents.

When planning a user research project, the research plan should document the systematic steps shown in Figure 5-1. The remainder of the chapter reviews these steps.

Figure 5-1. *Planning user research (Savarit, 2019)*

Determine the Aim of the Research Project

It is imperative to make a clear statement that contains the aim of the research project. Only then will you be able to start drafting your research questions.

Planning the research is essential, and it will save you a lot of time in the long run. I read several UX books that try to explain how to plan your research, but I didn't see much information regarding the aim of the project. They tend to jump straight to the questions and choosing the methods they will use to collect data.

Having a clear sentence that covers the aim of your research project will simplify the description of what you are trying to do.

Sometimes, when I am running a workshop with stakeholders, I ask them to define in one sentence what they are trying to do with their project. They often start with a long explanation, which for me does not make any sense as they are using jargon. Sometimes they repeat what other stakeholders are saying, and you realize that they do not know what all those techie words mean. I ask them to break down their description and make it simpler, like they were talking to a friend, their husband, or their wife, who does not know anything about the subject matter.

Having a clear and straightforward account of what you are trying to do is the recipe for creating a good plan.

The aim of a research project may depend on what development phase you are in. In a discovery phase, your research project aims at understanding the users who will be using the service or product, as well as identifying their needs. This should also be adapted to the subject and the context. For example, in the case of wanting to develop a new service for teachers, you want to know the following:

- Who will be using the service? It may not be the teacher; it may be someone else. It could be a teacher, head teacher, support team, admin team, etc.

- You will only find this out by asking yourself the question and by asking people who have expertise in this area to help you define who your audience is. If they are using a current service, your user research project would aim at understanding who the end user is who will be using the new service.

- Try to understand their current behavior and their opinion regarding the current service to help them identify the user needs. This is to inform the team of what needs to be done.

- This will identify what the current situation is and will help to decide whether a new service is needed; it can also get a clear account of the end users as well as their needs and what the new service could bring to them, as well as how the new service will impact them.

- Or, if they already use a service, how are they using the current service, and how can you make sure the possible new service that you want to build or improve will meet the user needs?

- Keep in mind that the stakeholders and product owner already have in mind what they want to build. To be clear, if you're going to be user-centered, it is essential that even if you are planning to develop a new service or redesign your website, you have to understand the user needs first.

- That doesn't mean you have to follow everything that comes from the research. I can't stress enough that a great and successful product or service needs to have the right balance between the user needs and the business needs. Nevertheless, I will emphasize that to get this right balance, you have to collect data with real users that will give an account of who the users are and their needs. As mentioned in Chapter 4, Samsung realized that people think of a television set as a piece of furniture, not as a piece of electronics.

- A lot of products have been developed based on market research; there is a big difference between market research and user research. As user researchers, we try to understand how somebody will use a digital product or service.

Understanding the user needs does not mean forgetting about the business needs; you may want to change providers, dematerialize the process to reduce cost, or offer a self-serve service that will enable you to close offices/agencies. Let's review a few examples.

Example 1: Redesigning a WebSite for Postgraduate Courses

The aim of the project is to have a better understanding of prospective/future postgraduate applicants and list what is important (information availability) to them to make their decision to apply to a program.

Example 2: Integrating Data into Your Current Financial Platform

Your company just bought a new company that provides commodities data, and you want to integrate the data into your current financial platform. Your project aims to understand who the users of commodities data are and understand what needs to be done to make sure the data provided will meet their needs.

Example 3: Redesigning an Intranet

The project will aim to understand what the business is trying to do by redesigning their company intranet, to identify the different types of users, and to identify which information and tools they are currently using and the type of information they are looking for on the intranet.

In the alpha phase, your research aims to evaluate the different solutions. You should already know who your users are; you can refine and identify more user types. We used to call this a *proof of concept*.

In the beta phase, your project aims to build the service or the product; the research project aims to have a clear account of your users and evaluate the end-to-end user journey.

Once your product is live, the aim of your project may vary: it could be to evaluate how your current service is doing or try to find out why you do not have enough traffic or interest in certain products. Once you have the aim of the research project, you can start creating the research questions you want to address.

You can always start with high-level research questions such as the following:

- Who are the users?

- What do you want to find out?

- What is the purpose of your service?

- What are the needs of the end users?

- What type of information do users need to complete the task?

- What are the blockers?

- What is the current client satisfaction?

- What do they think of the current website?

- How many people are visiting your website?

- How many transactions do you get monthly?

- How are they using the current service?

- How does the current service meet their user needs?

- How could a new service help the end users get a more natural journey?

- Why are they using the service?

- Why is there less traffic on your website?

- Why do some users not complete their transaction?

- Which type of information are users looking for?

Choosing the Relevant Method for Your Research

Once you have a list of high-level research questions, it will be easier for you to choose your research methodology. I want to differentiate research methodology from the method of collecting data. Currently many UXers do not make differentiate between the two.

The research methodologies can be separated into two approaches, quantitative and qualitative. The quantitative method is a bottom-down approach, starting with a hypothesis and trying to validate it. This starts with some pre-existing ideas, or theories, and uses a large sample size and statistical research methods, answering the questions how much and how often. (See Chapter 1.)

The qualitative method is a bottom-up approach, which is based on collecting data through observation, talking with real people, and answering the questions of why and how.

To get a full vision of what is going on, I recommend using mixed research methods. For example, in a discovery phase, you may look at analytics as a starting point, which is quantitative; then if you realize that the analytics are showing some unpredicted traffic, you can use qualitative research methods to understand why.

Again, the methods to collect data are different from the research method that you are using. The approach to collecting your data is not the way you are going to analyze the data.

Collecting Data and Equipment

You can use several methods to collect data. You can use a form, set up analytics on your platform to gather the traffic, create a survey, take a video of an interview, take notes while observing participants using a website, use some software to collect data (for example, first-click studies), record screens and audio and video, or even do eye tracking. User testing is a method to collect data; once you have your data, you need to analyze it; see Chapter 6 for the details of all the methods.

Figure 5-2 provides a brief account of methods to collect data.

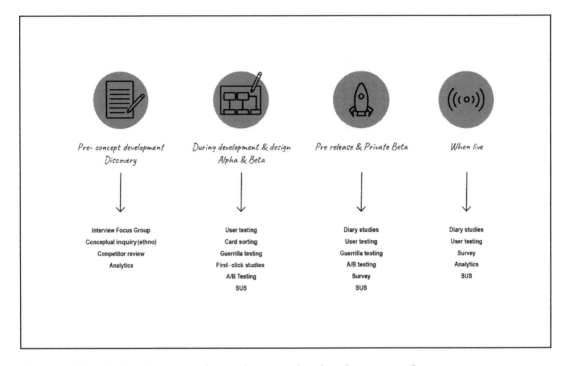

Figure 5-2. *Methods to use depending on the development phase*

You will choose your research method (quantitative or qualitative), depending on the research questions. After that, you can select the method to collect the data.

The following sections explain the methods that we generally use in accordance with the phase in which you are.

Discovery Phase

You will look at what you already know and then fill the gaps. Often this is a fieldwork phase, which includes using interviews, contextual inquiries, focus groups, desk work such as competitor reviews, and analytics if you have them.

Alpha

You may start by doing some user testing (via guerrilla testing rather than in a lab), card sorting exercises, first-click studies, or any of the methods from the discovery phase.

Beta

You will do more user testing here.

Private Beta

The diary study, as well as previous methods, is used in this phase.

Live

When your product is live, analytics are the way to monitor what is going on.

Equipment

There is no limitation to the type of equipment you can use to conduct your research. Here are some common things you might need:

- Paper
- Pen
- Online forms
- Discussion guides
- Software to do card sorting, first-click studies, video recordings, eye tracking
- Computers
- Prototypes
- Screens/design
- Sketches
- Video camera
- Sticky notes
- Sharpies

The equipment has changed a lot over the last few years. Before, we needed to rent a lab to get the screen capture, recordings, viewing rooms, or eye-tracking. Now we've got everything on our laptop; we can even stream the session live and give access to our colleagues via a link. We also used a video camera and filmed people interacting. It used to be much more archaic to conduct user research ten years ago when the equipment took up so much space, and it was also costly.

As a user researcher, we need to keep an eye on what is available on the market and always try new things.

Ethics

For the last ten years, I have emphasized the importance of ethics to people working in the field of user research. I can see that it is changing slightly, but still, on a number of occasions, I have seen some researchers not taking this issue very seriously. When collecting data with people, we need to respect some code of ethics and conduct.

"Researchers should respect the rights and dignity of participants in their research and the legitimate interests of stakeholders such as funders, institutions, sponsors and society at large" (BPS, 2014).

"*Research ethics* refers to the moral principles guiding research from its inception through to completion and publication of results" (BPS, 2014).

Principles

Here are four principles to follow while doing user research:

- Respect the participant's autonomy, privacy, and dignity.
- Scientific integrity.
- Social responsibility.
- Maximize benefits and minimize harm.

For more information, I invite you to look at the British Psychological Society's code of conduct.

Risks

Part of ethics is to consider the possible risk of what the research could do to the participant.

"Risk can be defined as the potential physical or psychological harm, discomfort or stress to human participants that a research project may generate" (BPS, 2014).

We, as researchers, have a responsibility to protect our participants from any discomfort. I will also emphasize this point to vulnerable people. What do I mean by vulnerable people? This refers to older people, children, or people with any disabilities (physical, cognitive, psychological).

For example, when you recruit participants who are on benefits because of their condition, they could be categorized as vulnerable if you are testing a product or service that they will be using to claim their benefit.

As an example, once some researchers went to do a home visit to collect data with someone who was retired and needed to test a service. After 30 minutes into the session, the participant felt tired and asked to stop the session. One of the researchers was not very pleased and wanted to continue the session as they needed the data for their research. The second researcher, who was a bit more experienced and knew that pursuing the testing would mean crossing the line of ethics and the code of conduct, told the other researcher that they needed to stop. I heard that the first researcher was not so happy and asked not to be charged for the recruitment of the participant. Remember that every participant has the right to withdraw at any time during the research. This should be respected.

Risk also could be for the researcher.

Participants with Psychological Conditions

Once I was doing a user testing session in a lab for a government project. I could see that a participant was a bit tense, and we knew he had some psychological conditions. We recruited this participant because we wanted to test the user journey with all different types of users. I could see the participant was unhappy and upset, and he started to be verbally violent with me; we could see his behavior was a bit risky. I have a lot of experience conducting research with people with his condition, and I did not feel uncomfortable about it. Still, I was cautious. I managed to get the participant to cooperate, and I earned his trust, which helped to change his behavior. At the end of the session, my team, which was in the viewing room, told me that they wanted to stop the session on several occasions as they thought it was not safe for me.

I was alright as I knew I had the team in the room next door, but how many times does it happen that no one is in the viewing room? I will always recommend that someone be close by, in the room next door.

Safety and Home Visits

I have had several arguments with the people who have been on the user researcher Community group channel. I mentioned that it is not safe for researchers to go on their own to do a home visit to collect data despite resistance from the leadership team; it seems now to be a bit more standard to have someone accompany the researcher on a home visit. I am glad that Stephanie Marsh, who works at GDS, also mentions the safety of the researcher in her book.

Here are the general rules of safety written by Cat Fox in our Gov user research channel:

- Give members of your team the address of where and who you are visiting and the times.

- Send regular check-ins and updates so that your team knows you are safe, especially if you are conducting several home visits in one day.

- Take the same approach if it is also where the participant is working.

- Never agree to meet a participant in a place that is not public or in a place where other people are not present, even if that request seems very innocent.

The standard rule here is if for any reason you feel uncomfortable, make an excuse and leave; do not question your instincts.

Consent

I want to start with the difference between giving consent and signing a nondisclosure agreement. Giving consent is done by the participant who allows us, researchers, to collect data and to use it. A nondisclosure agreement is for the participant to agree not to share any of the information that was made available during the session.

It is essential that user researchers ask for consent. First, they need to explain what the research is about and why we are looking for the participant to take part in it. If you are conducting remote testing, I recommend you send the consent form before the session. Then ask the participant to send it back to you. If you are recording the session, it is always useful to video record the consent.

You have to ask the participant permission to record the audio and video of the session. You need first to have the consent for recording the session, but you also need consent to use the data, quote, audio, and video clips. You need to make sure you get permission to share the data internally, as well as at conferences. If you do not have consent, you can't use it. I have seen so many clips and extracts used at UX events. I did not want to be a pain and ask if they had full consent…but I doubt it!

If you are doing the session in a lab or if you are streaming the session, you have to tell your participant that other people will be watching the session. If they disagree, you have to ask people to leave the viewing room or stop the streaming.

This should be clear and explained to the participant. You should not use data if you don't have consent.

The data should be kept securely, and just the researchers should have access to it. I've seen people sharing video data on Slack, Teams, and Google Drive. I am a bit concerned by this. There is no proper user research society that gives guidance to user researchers.

When getting consent from vulnerable people such children, you should get the consent from the parent as well as from the child; for people with cognitive impairment or any other disability, you need to make sure they have a full understanding of what you are doing; for people with disabilities, a caretaker may need to give consent.

You should also separate the participant consent from the data and change any names so that the data remains anonymous and to protect the identity of the participants.

Figure 5-3 shows an example of a consent form.

You have volunteered to participate in our User Research testing program. Prior to this, we need
you to complete and return this consent form. If you have any questions, please contact us at:
[youremail@example.com].

Project Title
TPO intranet Alpha

Invitation
You are being asked to take part in a research program to help design and create a new intranet service

What Will Happen
In this study, you will be asked to interact with screens, or website prototype.
The aim of the study is to evaluate how you interact with them. As part of the study you will be asked
to complete some tasks. There is not right answer: we are simply interested in your views on the site
and how easy you find it to use.

Time Commitment
The study typically takes around 45 minutes.

Participant's Rights
You may withdraw from the study at any time without having to give explanation.
You have the right to refuse to answer any questions if it makes you feel unconfortable.
If you have any questions regarding this research, we will answer it at the end of the session.

Confidentiality / Anonymity
We will collect your name, age, email address and telephone number for future contact as well
as for follow-up study were necessary. Your data will be used to classify the feedback we get from
the research. We may also refer to your first name in our final report.
If you prefer, we can anonymise you : just tell us during t he session.Video, audio and screen
activities and gaze will be used only for research purposes and will not be use on the public domain.
We will ask for your consent before using any recordings for conferences or publications.

For Further Information
Our researcher [name of the researcher here] will be happy to answer any questions you may have.
You may contant her at [youremail@example.com].By signing below, you are agreeing that :
[1] You have read and understood the consent form,
[2] questions about your participation in this study have been answered sarisfactorily,
[3] you are taking part in this reseaerch study voluntarily
[4] you are waving your right to request that we destroy any feedback from you during the process.

Participants's Name (Printed)*

Participant's signature*   Date

Name of person obtaining consent (Printed)   Signature of person obtaining consent

*Participants wishing to preserve some degree of anonymity may use their initials

Figure 5-3. *Consent form*

Recruiting Participants and Incentives

One of the most challenging parts of conducting user research is to recruit the right participants.

Conducting a user testing session with the wrong participants is a waste of time and money.

Many companies have staff members conduct tests and research and think that everyone is the user. This is, in my opinion, a risk that I will not take when I conduct user research. Internal staff members are biased despite their best intentions. Furthermore, internal staff may not reflect the behavior of real users. They may not be objective; also, you will miss out entirely on the people who are not computer savvy or have never used your product.

You don't always need to use a recruitment agency or pay for a panel. First, you need to have a clear idea of which participant you want for your researcher. I recommend creating a screener who will help you or the recruitment agency to recruit the right people.

Figure 5-4 provides an example of recruiting participants for an online iPad travel booking agent.

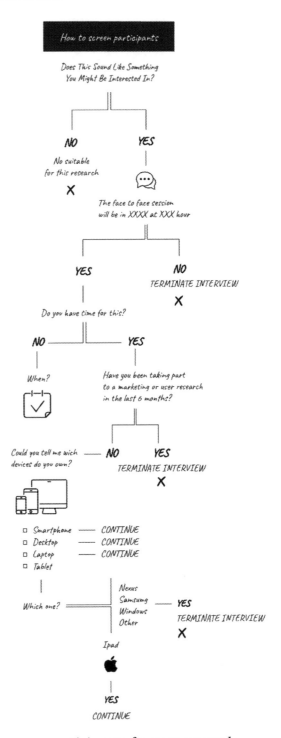

Figure 5-4. *How to screen participants for user research*

Using a recruitment agency is expensive, but sometimes it is necessary, especially if you do not have the resources in-house to help with the recruitment. Furthermore, when participants are difficult to find, I recommend you contact different participant recruitment agencies to get some quotes and to provide them with the information shown in Figure 5-5 to get a quote.

Here are the details for our testing requirements:

1. Type of testing - Lab Based testing
2. Number of participants - 10
3. Duration of test - around 1 hour per user.
4. Duration of the entire usability test - 1-2 days
5. Timeline of the test - Week of October 23
6. Type of participants - Freelance Electricians/
   Electricians working for small to large scale companies /
   Facility Managers. We will help finding some of our customers as participants.
7. Incentive £50
8. Devices used, iPhone, android, tablet

Figure 5-5. *Participant requirements for research*

Using a panel is cheaper, but it may provide only those people who spend a lot of time taking part in studies, user research, and marketing just for the incentive.

When you are doing qualitative research, I think it is essential to have real people taking part in the study.

I always try to recruit the participants myself, unless they are too difficult to recruit or if I do not have the time or the resources to help me.

Using Social Media

We needed some students to take part in user testing; the client wanted to pay a recruitment agency to get the participants, which would have cost between £50 and £75 ($65 to $100 USD) per participant plus £10 ($13 USD) voucher as an incentive. I asked my two children to post on their social media, "Looking for participants for remote user testing; compensation £20 ($26 USD) Amazon voucher." We got 30 participants in 48 hours.

Posting a Survey on Twitter

We needed to send a survey to teachers; the marketing department could not send an email to them as they do not want to over-solicit them. We came up with the idea to post the survey on Twitter with a hashtag; every member of staff retweeted the post and asked their friends to do the same with the hashtag. It worked; we got 950 answers in less than one week.

Use Your Network

We needed small business participants. As a member of the chamber of commerce I have access to a list of members, and some of them are small businesses. I sent them an email to ask them if they would be interested in taking part. I got replies from tailors, hairdressers, and startups. You can also use LinkedIn and other networks.

Use Your Client's List

Sometimes you may already have a list of your customers; you can have a junior staff member or a research assistant help you with the recruitment. It is too much for the user researcher to handle the recruitment as well as all the preparation of the research itself.

Use a Recruitment Agency

A recruitment agency typically costs between £50 to £95 ($65 to $145 USD) per participant depending on the profile. Figure 5-6, Figure 5-7, and Figure 5-8 provide three examples. You will have to create a clear description of the user you are looking for, as well as a management fee. They generally offer to prepare the screener for you. They can also manage the incentive for you probably with an extra charge for the management. Incentives may vary; depending on the participant, it could take as little as £20 ($26 USD) or up to £150 ($200 USD) if they are high-value professionals (e.g., traders, business journalists, etc.). Stephanie Marsh (2019) said, "It is well-spent money."

Niche User Reasearch Cost Model	Cost in GBP (£)*	Notes
Lab hire	£1000 - £1500 per day (depending on location)	To cover lab hire when supplier also recruiting participants as well as provision of a lab where (company name) recruit participants themselves
Incentive (per user)	£40 - £ 70 depending on the participant £10 (handling fee)	To cover all participant types (please show range that would be paid for different user type, if applicable). Please also confirm if a handling fee is charged

* all prices excluding VAT

Figure 5-6. *Example of recruitment agency cost 1*

Niche User Reasearch Cost Model	Cost in GBP (£)*	Notes
Assisted digital participant- Niche (cost per user)	£65 (85$)	
Project managment cost (cost per job/recruitment request)	£100 (130$) **per job**	Supplier to confirm if they change a flat rate per job
	£100 (130$) **per screener**	NB we also need to know if there is any one-off set up cost over and adobe this (if so, we expect this to be for niche only and by negotiation)

* all prices excluding VAT

Figure 5-7. *Example recruitment agency cost 2*

Niche User Reasearch Cost Model	Cost in GBP (£)*	Notes
Standard participant (cost per user)	£65 (85$)	
Assisted digital participant (cost per user)	£70-£80 (90-110)	Senior citizen and English as a second language : £70 (90$) ⸻ Motor and cognitive disability, mental health condition: £80 (90$)
Standard participant - Niche (cost per user)	£70 (90$)	

* all prices excluding VAT

Figure 5-8. *Example recruitment agency cost 3*

I recommend that you hire different agencies specializing in recruitment. Large organizations generally subcontract with smaller specialized agencies. If you are doing a lot of user research, it is good to invest in a research assistant who could help you with the recruitment and build your own recruitment capabilities in-house.

Incentives

It is easier to get participants if you are giving an incentive; you can offer a cash incentive, or you can give Amazon or iTunes vouchers. You can also provide the option to donate to a charity or give a bottle of wine. I have done this with traders who came to the Thomson Reuters (TR) lab; we gave them the option of £150 cash, giving to a charity, or getting six bottles of wine. See Figure 5-9.

Incentives	Cost in GBP (£)*
30-minute session	£30 GBP (40 $)
45-minute session	£45 GBP (60 $)
60-minute session	£60 GBP (80 $)

* all prices excluding VAT

Figure 5-9. *Incentives*

Whether you use an agency or not, you have to plan your session. Sometimes to get your participants, you need to have an off-hours testing session.

Scheduling Your Session

Allow enough time between sessions and also a lunch break for the researcher. So many times no one has thought I would need a break during the day! (See Chapter 6.)

Analyzing

Analyzing your data may vary depending on the approach you will be taking. If it is a survey, you can probably ask the online survey software to calculate your results. With analytics, it is the same, but you could also export the raw data into Excel or SPSS to do your analysis (Figure 5-10).

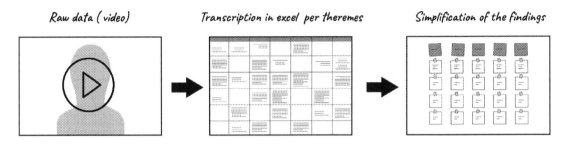

Figure 5-10. Process of analysis

For qualitative approaches, the most common way to analyze data is to do a thematic analysis, looking for common themes in your data.

I highly recommend going back to the data or audio and video file (see Chapter 6 for more details). I will use sticky notes only at the end of the analysis. Some researchers tend to jump directly to the sticky note session or even analyze with the team without going back to the data (Figure 5-11). I will explain the risk of using this approach in the next chapter. The analysis is the most critical phase; it takes time, but often not enough time is not allocated to conduct a proper analysis.

Figure 5-11. Sticky note findings

Once you have all your results and have extracted the main findings, it is time to share them with your team and the stakeholders.

Presenting and Sharing Your Findings

The presentation of your findings may differ depending on your audience, the phase you are in, and how you work in your team. I recommend these three ways to share your findings:

- Highlight findings in a short document to share with your team

- Create a few slides for show-and-tell

- Create a full presentation

Overview/Highlight Findings

If you are in a beta phase and are conducting user testing every sprint, you won't have the time to prepare a full presentation at every show-and-tell. I recommend preparing after every user testing session a short A4 document covering the main findings (Figure 5-12) to share with your team.

Figure 5-12. *Overview/high-level findings*

Short Presentation

If you have a session with some stakeholders or a show-and-tell if you haven't finished the research, I recommend two to three slides that include the following information (Figure 5-13):

- What the research session was about

- Participants

- Main findings so far

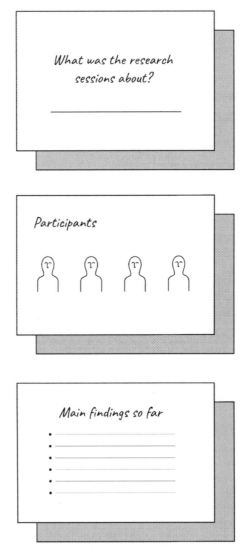

Figure 5-13. *Short presentation*

Report Presentation

Make a clear presentation of your findings. Before starting to write it, try to find out who will be reading it or who will be present the day you will be presenting your results. This will help you to design a presentation that will be targeted to your audience. Try not to overcrowd the slides; the minimalist style tends to be better. In terms of content, avoid jargon; the audience may not understand it.

Graphs, infographics, quotes, and audio or even video clips could be a good idea.

Organizing Your Work and Storing Data

I find that folders of user researchers can become messy quickly. Sometimes when you ask a content writer or a designer to give you the last version of their work, it is not always easy to get it. It's the same with user researchers; our documents can become very messy. It is hard sometimes to find the relevant documents; we have to deal with so many of them. This is why now every time I start a new project, I follow the same organization. I also do the same when I start working at client sites. Whatever structure they are using, I apply the same organization so it is easy to find information, documents, etc. (Figure 5-14).

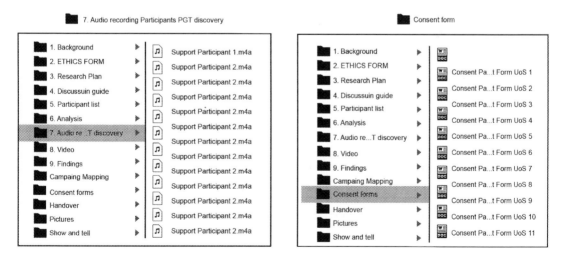

Figure 5-14. *User research folder organization*

I create a new folder with the name of the project; then I create subfolder, as shown here:

Folder 1: Background Information

In this folder you should put all the document of previous research and reports that may be useful for this research.

Folder 2: Research Plan

Research questions: This is the document in which you have drafted all the research questions for your research.

Hypothesis: The hypothesis needs to be written in simple words so you can refer to it later.

Folder 3: Material/Equipment

Discussion guide: A discussion guide is a document with the list of questions that the researcher will ask through the session (interview, user testing, etc.).

Questionnaire: A questionnaire is a set of questions with predefined answers.

Prototype: A prototype is one of the first simplified versions of the product that you want to build.

Screens: They show the early design of what will be part of the prototype, or part of the build product.

Tools: This is a list of all the equipment that you will require for your research; it could include video camera, notebook, diary, hardware, etc.

Software: This is the software that you are using for your research. Some people may use Zoom to record a remote session; it could be also a survey software, etc.

Folder 4: Participants

Ethics: This contains all the consent forms signed by the participants. You need to keep them until you have completed the research. If you plan to use some of the data, you should keep the consent forms.

Participant list: This is an Excel document with the participant details, demographics, and other information collected before the research.

Screener: The screen capture is the set of questions that is helping to recruit the relevant participants.

Email/letter: If you send an introduction email to your participants, all the correspondence needs to be kept in this folder.

Incentive: This is all the information related to the incentive; if it is a cash incentive, participants need to sign a form about receiving it.

Other documents: This contains any other documents that you may have used for the research.

Folder 5: Data

Raw data: The raw data could be an Excel spreadsheet with all the survey data, the analytics, etc. The raw data also can be audio and video clips as well as pictures and notes.

Clips: You may use these for your presentation as evidence to support your findings.

Data management: If you have a lot of data, it is always good to have an Excel document that recaps all the data and links to where it is located.

Folder 6: Analysis

Excel: This contains several Excel documents in which you are doing your analysis, video analysis, questionnaire analysis, or web analytics analysis.

SPSS: If you are using SPSS, this contains the data and the analysis documents.

Pictures: Sticky notes help to simplify and extract the main findings of the analysis. Take a picture of them to keep in this folder, just in case you need to go back to it.

Etc.: This can contain any other document that may be useful such as SUS and other questionnaires, as well as the analysis of the system usability scale.

Folder 7: High-Level Findings

This is a small document in which you have all the highlight findings. This is a digestible document that you can go through quickly and also share with your team.

Folder 8: Presentation

This is the folder with your entire presentation for this project.

Systematically organizing your research makes it easy to retrieve any information in the future; also, other researchers can access the documents to make it easier for everyone.

The process of structuring your research is systematic, and you can replicate it for every research project you are doing. With a well-structured process and plan, you will save a lot of time, reuse the same structure, and also start creating your template. This organization can be applied to all projects, whatever methodology you are going to use.

Summary

Here are the key takeaways from the chapter:

- Planning research is essential.

- Documenting all the aspect of the research is useful, especially if you need to go back to the research in the future.

- Following a clear process, make your research structured and systematic.

- Organizing all your documents in a clear format may save you and your peers a lot of time.

CHAPTER 6

Research Methods: Analytics, Surveys, and Card Sorting

Often user research is associated with usability. User research uses several methods to collect and analyze data. As mentioned in the previous chapter, it is fundamental to start drafting the research questions before choosing your research method (Nunnally & Farkas, 2016). Once you have them, you can choose the right research method to answer them.

- **The quantitative research method** takes a top-down approach, starting with the big picture and using deductive reasoning.

  Quantitative research methods require a large sample, involve a large amount of data, and are associated with experimental research, analytics, survey, etc. The quantitative approach validates the hypotheses, theories, or preconceived ideas.

- **The qualitative research methods** take a bottom-up approach. They start from a specific observation to generalization and inform theory.

  Generally, qualitative research requires fewer participants (case studies, observations, interviews, etc.) The qualitative approach necessitates an in-depth investigation. Qualitative research identifies phenomena, common patterns, and systematic occurrences.

The format of the qualitative data in user research can include notes, pictures, audio, video, screen captures, and recordings. There are many research methods at our disposal. In this book, I am covering the ones that we use the most currently. This chapter will look at analytics, surveys, and card sorting. Chapter 7 will introduce you to user testing, ethnographic/contextual inquiries, interviews, and diary study.

© Emmanuelle Savarit 2020
E. Savarit, *Practical User Research*, https://doi.org/10.1007/978-1-4842-5596-4_6

Analytics

Analytics collects data on any digital platform (website). Analytics captures activities that occur when people are using a platform. This generates quantitative data, and generally analytics produces a large amount of data.

Analytics helps to gather and quantify the activity, traffic, bounce rate, click-through rate, number of new visitors, and transaction completion/conversion rates on your website. Spinutech's website gives a good overview of what matters the most in terms of analytics: "If you have a live product, it is a starting point before doing any user research about the current situation. It helps you to prepare your research plan." Farkas & Nunnaly (2017) said that "analytics helps to make sense of the mess."

The following are some questions that analytics answers:

- How many people visited your website?

- Which pages did they go to?

- How long did they stay on your website?

- How many transactions were completed, and what was the order size (this is important for e-commerce)?

- How long did it take someone to complete the transaction?

- What is the location of the audience?

Tools to Collect the Data

A large organization may have its own department of analysts who can extract data on demand. You have to tell them what you are looking for. For example, you might want to know how many people visited your site or a specific section of your site daily, weekly, monthly, etc. Now it is easy to set up the analytics of your website with tools such as Google Analytics, Adobe Analytics, Big Picture, and Matomo.

Sometimes companies haven't set their analytics on their site or some of their platforms. A lack of analytics makes it impossible to find out how their platform is performing.

If you realize that you haven't set up analytics, it is never too late. I recommend planning your analytics as soon as you start building a platform. It is worth getting the help of a specialist. If you feel confident about doing it yourself, though, there are many tools to collect analytics. The most popular one is Google Analytics (Figure 6-1). This solution captures the activity of your website and is also relatively easy to use.

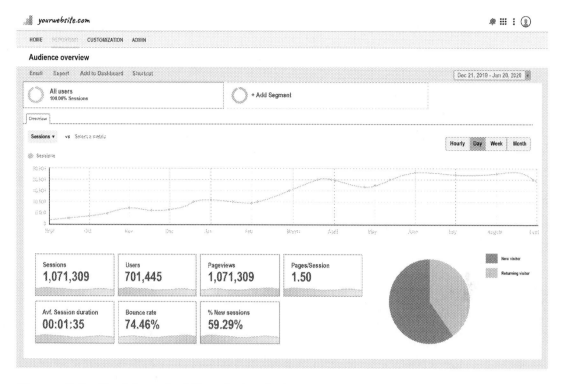

Figure 6-1. *Dashboard of Google Analytics*

Analyzing the Data

To analyze data, you can rely on the analysis done by Google Analytics or similar tools. If you have the raw data and want to be a bit more rigorous, you can clean the data. Cleaning data means making sure you do not have false responses or corrupted data. For example, you may be accessing your site to create some tests so your data is not data from real users. By removing data with your own work IP address, you are cleaning your data.

Some analytics providers may offer to complete the analysis of your data; you can use them to provide you with the analysis and get some graphs. You can also get the raw data and export it into Excel, make a list of the variables in which you are interested, and then calculate the sum, average, and mean.

You can calculate the total number of page views, for example, and then divide the sum by the number of users that will give you the average page views per users. You can use Excel and calculate the sum, the average, and the percentage of the traffic. Excel can also provide you with graphs that you can use in your final report.

Interpreting the Data

Once you have analyzed your data, you can evaluate and interpret the findings by asking and answering a series of questions, beginning with the following initial research questions:

- How many people visited your site?

  For example, we had [x] visitors this month, but last month we had fewer visitors during the school holidays.

  You can also see the sum of the visits as well as calculating the average visit per day/month.

- Which pages did they go to?

  You can create a list of the most visited pages and identify the content that attracts the most users. For instance, it could be My Account, the contact page, or My Cart. If the analytics show that there is a lot traffic on the contact page, it is a red flag that something is going on. You need to try to understand why people are going to this page. It is a starting point to investigate more.

  Moreover, try to identify where users go next: do they send an email, or if you have a contact form, do they complete the form? What is the topic of their inquiry? Do they call? Do they go to the FAQ section if you have one?

- How long did they stay on your website?

  The average time spent on a website is around two minutes; this is long enough for the visitor to read the content and also to complete a transaction. It also depends on the type of service or product you are offering. For example, for grocery shopping, it takes more than two minutes to fill up a shopping basket. The next time you are going online to read an article, try to capture how long you stay on the site. Do the same when making a purchase. How long did it take you to buy something on Amazon or similar? How long does it take you to do your grocery shopping online? The critical approach is to be objective and evaluate what is the average time you are expecting visitors to stay on your website.

- How many transactions were completed? What was the order size? (This is important for e-commerce.)

  You can also capture the amount of completed transactions through your site; this is important for your marketing team. What would interest the user researchers is to evaluate how to improve the transaction journey and make it faster and simpler. Therefore, the completion rate could be used as a baseline to look at before and after improving the design, architecture, navigation, or user journey. Evaluating how much time people are spending on average can also help to add some characteristics to the persona representing your clients/users.

- How long did it take them to complete the transaction?

  We know that a long user journey to complete a transaction increases the chance of the user leaving your site prematurely and therefore not completing the transaction. Understanding how long it takes to complete your transaction may also provide you with some insight that indicates that you need to improve your user journey and experience. All users now expect to complete transactions quickly.

- Where is the audience located?

  The localization of your visitor may have an impact on your business decisions. Imagine that you are an e-commerce business and shipping some goods. The other day, I was in Santa Monica, having a coffee, and the person next to me started talking to me. She was the owner of a doughnut shop on Montana Avenue, Santa Monica. I started chatting with her, and she explained that she preferred having a client in California. As Shipping doughnuts outside the California were adding a significant expense. Maybe, in the long run, identifying the localization of her clients would encourage her to open another shop if it was more cost-effective in comparison to her shipping costs.

- Which devices are used by users?

Identifying which devices your users are using is critical information when you design a website, app, or platform. If your audience is always on the go, make sure your product is usable on mobile devices. The device analytics provides you with valuable information. Also, note the difference between the Android and iPhone platform sizes. I once tested a new banking app for a client in Hong Kong. The prototype was for iPhones, but when I arrived in Hong Kong, I took the subway, and I could not see anyone with an iPhone. Also, the screen that they were using was much bigger than the one we were using in Europe. Identifying at an early stage which devices clients/users use enables you to identify the right target audience for your user testing sessions.

Presenting

To present analytics findings, I recommend making beautiful graphs (see the examples in Figure 6-2 through Figure 6-6). This can be achieved with Excel or Number (Apple), or if you have a design team, you can ask them to make some great graphs.

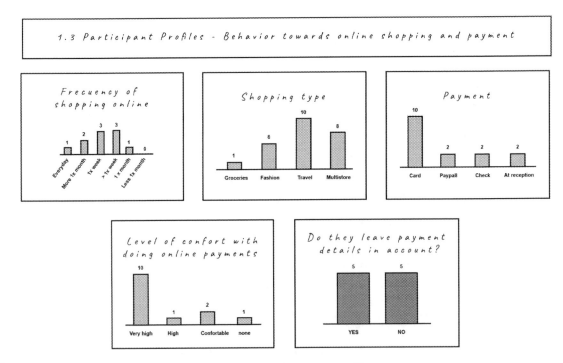

Figure 6-2. *Presentation analytics, participant profiles 1*

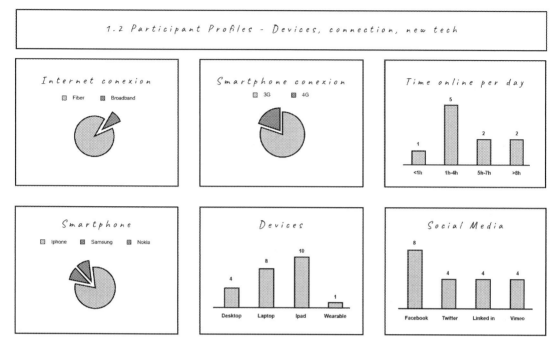

Figure 6-3. *Presentation analytics, participant profiles 2*

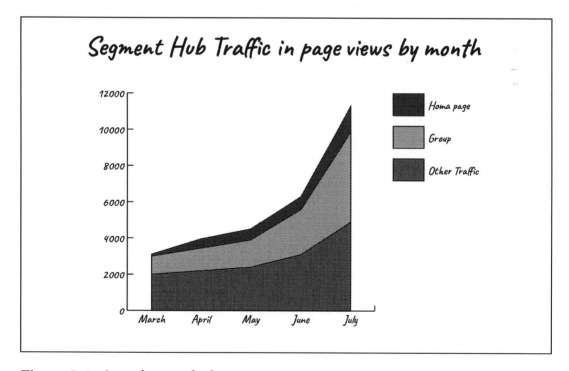

Figure 6-4. *Sample growth chart*

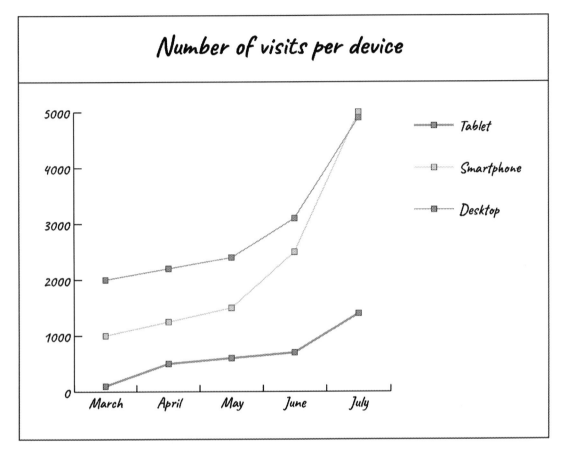

Figure 6-5. *Number of visits per device and per month*

Annual review 2012 - Overview

Annual review traffic

. 20% of investors traffic (was 3% of investors traffic in the prev 4 weeks)

. 5,100 unique visitors

. 7,185 visits

. 6.8 Pages/ visit (vs. 3.7 Pages/ Visiti for overall Investor's traffic)

. Avg visit duration - 7m 11s (vs. 4m 33s for overall Investor's traffic)

. 803 Annual Review PDF dowloaded (11% of visits included a download)

. 4,788 Annual Report PDF downloaded (67% of visits included a download)

. 262 downloaded both reports

. 29 Annual report documents downloaded from the app

Audience segment

Investors

Media

?

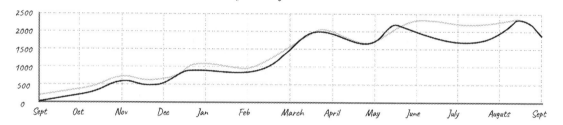

Figure 6-6. *Sample traffic graph*

While presenting your analytics findings, you should be clear and precise. You do not want to overwhelm the audience with too much information.

- State the aims of the project.

- State the methods and the purpose of the analytics.

- Explain where the data comes from (e.g., we looked at the last three months of activity of your website).

- Which tool did you use to collect the data (e.g., Google Analytics)?

- You need to restate the research questions and why you are asking those questions. (How many people visited the website? How many people completed a purchase? Where is the client located?)

- Then you can present the findings in relation to the research questions.

- After each result, you should explain in plain English what the results mean. What are the issues? Do you have enough information to make a decision? Or do you need to continue the research to understand why?

- Do not forget to flag the limitations of your findings, such as you did not have enough data or any technical issues that may have affected the data.

- You need to restate the research questions to make sure your audience understands what you were investigating.

- You should also try to find out who will be reading your report or attending your presentation. Make sure that all your data is labeled. Try to use a good size font, lovely colors, and good contrast for everyone to read it. Don't forget to take into consideration visually impaired people such as the color-blind. I recommend using the company branding presentation. It is also essential to explain in simple words what the numbers mean in the context of the business.

Analytics Conclusion

User researchers need to have access to analytics. We can also help the data team to identify which analytics tool provides the relevant data to assess your new product. As a user researcher, I always ask if any analytics are available; if so, I will look at them. Analytics gives me some context and helps me plan every project. It is a starting point for every research project.

Nevertheless, you have to keep in mind that analytics alone is not enough, and do now answer the questions of why, how, and who.

Surveys

Surveying is the most commonly used methodology across all fields of research including human-computer interaction (HCI), psychology, market research, sociology, etc. Surveying is generally used to describe a population (Lazar et al, 2014). A survey is a methodology that uses questionnaires to collect data. The format of the questionnaires could be paper, phone, or electronic, which is now the most frequent way to collect questionnaire responses. The questionnaire is completed by the users of your product or your clients.

A survey generally allows researchers to get factual information, such as trends, opinions, or the big picture of a specific population. Examples of surveys include government census, customer satisfaction, opinion, etc.

The advantage of conducting a survey is that you can get a large sample size that will validate some of your assumptions. In user research, surveying is not always the best method to use at the early stage of product development. It would be better if you already have a product live with a large number of users before conducting a survey. If you have enough users, the survey will give you answers to your questions related to how people interact with your product and services.

To reap the benefits of using a survey, you need to make sure the questions are well-written. Surveying often is used for the wrong reason: because it is an easy and inexpensive way to conduct research, not because it is the right method to collect the data that will answer your research questions.

Questions That a Survey Will Answer

A survey will answer questions related to characteristics, behaviors, or opinions.
It will also answer the following:

- Demographic questions such as gender, ethnicity, income, nationality, age, profession, and marital status

- Habits

- Opinions such as linking/disliking or frequency of usage

You can also find out the following:

- Which devices they are using, or which apps, websites, or software users are using

- How often they are using it

- How much they are ready to spend on a product

- When they are using it

You can also validate hypotheses; be careful with some random hypotheses or preconceived ideas.

I find that surveys are useful to validate findings from qualitative research. Creating a questionnaire based on phenomenon and systematic patterns that emerged from field research can be highly valuable. I have created a survey and sent it to a large sample to validate quantitative findings from qualitative research. It's not that I found the qualitative research findings not valid or reliable; I use a survey because stakeholders have difficulties understanding the value of qualitative data. Stakeholders seem to trust more quantitative results, probably because they are more familiar with statistics. Stakeholders may not realize that face-to-face interviews with 12 people are more reliable than a survey with 100 to 200 respondents. But that is another story!

Tools to Collect Data from a Questionnaire

Creating a questionnaire may be challenging for people without research backgrounds. A questionnaire needs to be well-written, without leading questions.

As no one will assist the respondent in completing the questionnaire, it is essential to make the questions easier to understand. You have the choice between open-ended questions, close-ended questions, or a combination of both.

Open-Ended Questions

Open-ended questions will take more time to analyze, especially if you have thousands of respondents. Open-ended questions will allow the respondent to think about their answers and to complete the answer. It will take the respondent more time to complete open-ended questions (Figure 6-7).

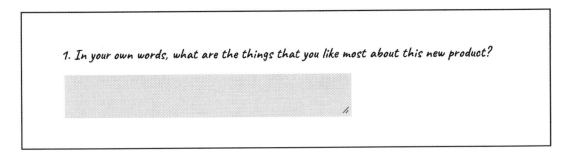

1. In your own words, what are the things that you like most about this new product?

Figure 6-7. *Open-ended question*

Close-Ended Questions

A close-ended question has a selection of prewritten answers. In comparison with the open-ended question, this one does not leave space for the respondent to provide a response with their own words. The respondent will have to select one or several prewritten answers. The following sections describe a few of the formats available for creating close-ended questions for user research.

Ranking

In this method, a respondent is asked to rank in order or preference devices by frequency of usage. In Figure 6-8, we are interested in the devices that our participants are using while watching video. The results will just give us an indication of which devices they use the most. Keep in mind that this will not tell us why.

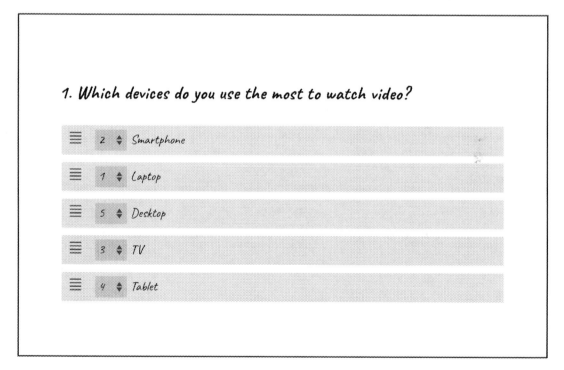

Figure 6-8. *Survey ranking question*

Likert Scale

The Likert psychometric scale is used to give a rating. There are different types of scales; the most widely used are five- and seven-point scales. Some researchers think that a nine-point scale is more reliable. I would say for user research, having five or seven points is good enough. In the example shown in Figure 6-9, we are asking the respondent to rate the quality of a product with a five-point scale.

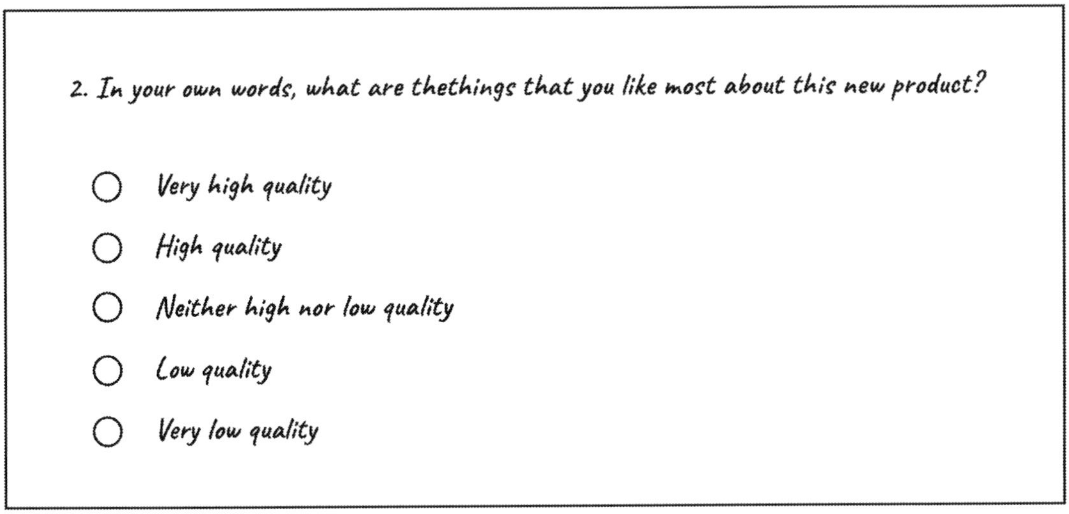

Figure 6-9. *Survey Likert scale*

Multiple Choice

This form of question requires the respondent to select the correct answer from a list of choices. In the example in Figure 6-10, we are asking the respondent to specify their job role.

3. What is your job role?

- ○ Product owner
- ○ Delivery manager
- ○ Developer
- ○ Tester
- ○ Designer
- ○ User researcher
- ○ Content designer
- ○ Bussiness analyst

Figure 6-10. *Survey, multiple choices*

You can use another format to design your questionnaire. The most important thing is to make sure your questions are not leading to any particular answer. Do not use negative words. Do not use words such as "Do you agree?" Ask only one question at the time; a common mistake is to ask two questions in one.

When you start designing you survey, do not forget to also provide the background or context, as well as the instructions. If you want a good response rate, inform from the start how many questions you will be asking and how long it should take to complete the survey. If you are not familiar with designing survey questionnaires, ask people with a research background to take a look at your questions, and ask them to give you some feedback. Some organizations have a market research or a social behavior research team; ask them to take a look at your questionnaire. Whatever field of research they have been studying, they should have enough knowledge to give you feedback.

Running a Pilot to Test Your Questionnaire

Running a pilot will help you to test your questionnaire and see how long it will take to complete it. Doing a pilot will help you to make sure you haven't missed any questions. The pilot aims to get feedback on the clarity of the questions, identify any errors, and evaluate the time it takes to complete the survey. Basically, doing a pilot gives you the opportunity to improve the questionnaire if needed before running the survey to a wider audience.

Paper, Online, or Phone Survey?

You can still use paper questionnaires; the problem is that it will be time-consuming to process the responses. You will need to know how to process them. It may also be difficult to read open-ended questions. Depending on the number of participants you have, a paper survey at the end of a user testing session may be easier to complete than completing a survey online at a later date. Using a paper survey is not ecological if you want to reduce paper use. You can also send a survey by mail, but this will use paper and envelopes as well as add postage cost. Also, you will need someone to add the addresses and take them to the post office or get them ready for postal collection. It will definitely add cost. Some participants may not be on the Internet, however, so if you have to capture feedback for a certain audience, it may be worth considering a postal survey.

Now, it is much more frequent to use online surveys. You send an email to your participant list, with the instructions and a link to the survey. To use online surveys there are so many tools available on the market. Here are examples of online survey tools: SurveyMonkey, Type Form, Survey Gizmo, etc. You can find a list of free software on Capterra's blog: `https://www.capterra.com/survey-software/`; Ross Rubin, in his June 2019 article in PCMag, also offers a comparison of several software applications.

A phone survey is also an option, but it may be time-consuming, and it is hard work. People are not always be nice to the researcher due to the large number of commercial phone calls that we receive nowadays. We can use AI to conduct the phone survey. This may be innovative; nevertheless, some participants do not like replying to a computer instead of a person. You can also use text messaging, which is less intrusive and permits the respondent to reply on his own time.

Bear in mind, however, that there are some issues with surveys. For example, a survey with too few responses will affect the reliability and validity of the results, so be sure to follow these guidelines:

- Explain the purpose of the survey in a simple language.

- Keep your survey short, 10–15 questions max.

- Tell your audience how many questions there are and how long it will take them to complete it.

- For postal surveys, provide a stamped return envelope.

- Offer an incentive such as a prize draw or raffle. (Once we offered an iPad in a prize draw, which I thought was a bit excessive, but at the end we got a large sample, so it was worth every penny.)

- Some audiences are solicited too often by email, so I find that posting on social media such as Twitter with the proper hashtag may work better. People who follow a topic will get the survey in their feed and will be more likely to respond.

- Try to get some influencers with many followers to retweet.

- You can also pay for a panel; this may be useful if you are looking for a specific audience that is difficult to reach.

Analyzing the Data

There are several ways to analyze your survey data. Before starting to analyze it, you need to clean the data. Like with analytics, it is important that the data is real and not corrupted. The researcher has to go through the data and verify if the answers are valid.

- Remove any respondent with an incomplete questionnaire.

- Remove any respondent where all the results are the same (all the results are number 5 of your five-point scale).

- If the same participants has done the same survey twice or more, remove them.

- Remove all the respondents who do not meet the sample criteria.

Once the data is cleaned, you can start the quantitative analysis. Statistical tools such as SPSS are used for complex surveys; you can also use Excel for simple questionnaires. Excel could be enough for user research survey questionnaires. Also, some survey software such as SurveyMonkey provides analysis and graphs. Once you have the analysis, it is important to interpret the results, or determine what the results mean in relation to your research questions. You also need to take into consideration the weaknesses of your results. Weaknesses could be not enough participants, too many people from the same age group, too many people in the same location, etc. Once you have the results, you need to step back. This helps you make sure that you interpret your results with objectivity. I have seen many people looking at the results without taking into consideration all the parameters just because the main trend was supporting their initial idea. Doing user research while developing a new digital product should be taken seriously. A lot of money is involved in the development of a digital product. You can't just jump straight to a conclusion without objectivity; the risk is too great.

Now it is time to analyze the open-ended questions. Don't forget to allocate time as you are going to do a qualitative analysis. A more detailed explanation will be in Chapter 9.

- Prepare an Excel document with all your open-ended questions and all the answers per participant.

- Read all the answers and start coding. I prefer doing a thematic analysis rather than a content analysis. I explain this in Chapter 9, but in short, we may not have the time or the resources to do a content analysis that requires a second coder. Thematic analysis is based on recurrent patterns in your data. For example, if the word *navigation* keeps coming back throughout the data, this will be a theme. You can color code it in green if it is a positive comment and in red if it is a negative comment.

- Then you can make a list of all the themes that you identified.

- Once you have the list, see how often a theme recurred in your data. Evaluate the impact of each theme on your product. Then relate the themes to your research questions. It may happen that something is emerging from your data that you haven't anticipated (I will talk more about it in Chapter 8).

Interpreting the Data

Once you have received the data, make sure you have enough respondents. I am not happy with any survey that gets fewer than 1,000 respondents. I understand that it is not always possible to get a high number of respondents, but aiming for it is a good start.

I will also take the time to look at the data, rethink my research questions, and see how the results answer the question.

Here's an example: Say we are creating a new iPad apps for children, and we are expecting users to use it for one hour a day. The entire business model is based on one hour of usage a day. One of the survey questions is: how much time do you allow your kid to spend on the iPad?

If the answer is 30 minutes a day, you will realize that there is an issue between business expectations and how much time parents will allow their child to play on an iPad daily. If you get the response 60 minutes a day, you may think that it is good, as it matches our business anticipated time of usage. Nevertheless, kids may also play games, watch cartoons, etc., which will reduce the time allocated to use your app. It is also important to allocate time to put the results in perspective.

When you interpret the findings, look at the following:

- Research questions

- Business needs

- Context

- Audience

- Age group

Presenting Survey Findings

Like in any research project, findings should follow the same format:

- State the aim of the project.

- State that you used the survey method and the advantages and the weaknesses of that method.

- Specify which audience you targeted and how you got them to respond.

- Specify which tool you used to collect the data (e.g., SurveyMonkey).

- You need to restate the research questions and why you are asking those questions. (How many minutes do you allow your kids to play with the iPad? Which games do your kids play with? Which design do you prefer? Which functionality do you prefer?)

- Then you can present the findings related to the research questions.

- After each result, you should explain in plain English what the results mean. What are the issues? How many respondents like the same design?

- Don't forget to flag the limitations of your findings, such as you did not have enough respondents or your data set was not diverse enough.

- You need to restate the research questions to make sure your audience understands what you were investigating.

- State both the full amount of respondent and then the percentage, for example:

  - Out of the 1,000 respondents, 675 prefer the blue design, 186 the green, 99 the red, and 40 the purple.

  - There is a clear preference for the blue design, which is 67.5 percent of the respondents.

- You should also try to find out who will be reading your report or attending your presentation. Make sure that all your data is labeled. Try to use a good size font, lovely colors, and good contrast for everyone to read it. Don't forget to take into consideration visually impaired people such as the color-blind. I recommend using the company branding presentation. It is also essential to explain in simple words what the numbers mean in the context of the business.

Surveys Conclusion

Surveying is sometimes overused, and many users get tired of being surveyed after using/buying a product. Surveying is overused in market research, which can affect survey responses. Nevertheless, if you want to use a survey to validate some findings and also ask some demographic questions, a questionnaire survey is easy, is fast, and is able to access a larger sample. I recommend using a survey for data validation.

Card Sorting

I would like to thank Jerome Ryckborst, who masters the card sorting method and who generously wrote the card sorting section. In a card-sorting study, you can find relationships between items by asking your intended readers to sort them into groups or categories that make sense to them. Each item is represented by a card. The categories that card-sorting reveals, and the names participants give to those categories, help you determine how to organize and label the information on a website or intranet. This organization and labeling is also called *information architecture* (IA).

For card sorting, you will typically use an online tool such as Optimal Workshop's Optimal Sort or UserZoom's Card Sorting.

The best time to use card sorting is when determining the IA of a website or intranet. The cards that participants sort can represent website topics, concepts and ideas, retail products, or any set of items you want your audience to be able to find. You can:

- Learn how to categorize the items and label those categories, by using an open card sort

- Confirm that the categories you provide make sense, by using a closed card sort

You can research all your site's content or just one section, or you can determine whether new items fit into your site's existing IA.

Note that card sorting does not explain *why* people prefer certain organizations, only *that they do*. This makes card sorting useful to predict reader performance, answering the questions:

- Where will our readers look for the information they need about a specific task or concept?

- How should we name the categories so our readers look in the right place for specific information?

- Does new information fit into the existing categories and labels?

The following sections explain the nuances of gathering the data, including which tools to use and how to get the participants.

The Basic Method

To begin, develop a set of cards and choose a card-sorting variant. Your schedule and budget will influence how much research you can do.

Provide a participant with cards that have terms or phrases written on them. Ask the participant to arrange the cards into categories that make sense to them. After repeating this with other participants, analyze the results to discover common groupings, or categories.

Repeat this process with the cards in one category to find its common subgroupings; then do this for each category until you have the data needed to organize and name the whole set of categories and subcategories, also called the IA.

Choosing the Card-Sorting Variant

You can choose open card sorting, closed card sorting, or a hybrid. For all variants, the cards to sort can be either specific items (information), the categories of information, tasks, or concepts.

Open Card Sorting

Use open card sorting to generate possibilities when you start designing a new information product or improving one you already have. Use open card sorting to learn the following:

- How readers understand and conceptualize the items in your set

- Where readers expect to find the items when they use your information product

- Whether different groups of readers use the same approach to finding items

- Ideas for organizing and labeling parts of your information product

Closed Card Sorting

Use closed card sorting to evaluate possibilities when you want to assess whether a given set of category names provides a helpful way to organize your content. Use closed card sorting to learn the following:

- Where new topics fit into an existing website or intranet

- Where category names are unclear

- Whether you can reduce the number of categories, by testing whether a smaller set still works well

Hybrid Card Sorting

Use hybrid card sorting in different ways. Depending on the categories you provide, hybrid card sorting can be more like a closed card sort or more like an open card sort.

If you provide fewer categories than your participants will need, they will be more likely to create new categories to complete the card sort. Do this to:

- Set the tone of the organizational pattern while encouraging participants to generate and name their own categories.

- Further explore groupings that were unclear in an earlier sort while providing categories for groupings that were clear.

- If you provide the categories that your participants need, they will be more likely to sort the cards into your categories only and less likely to create new categories. Do this to give participants:

  - A just-in-case option

  - An option for cards that they don't think fit well in the categories you provided

Creating the Cards and Categories

Each card must represent a concept or an item that your participants can successfully group. Build on what you already know about your readers, their motivations, their needs, and their tasks. A needs analysis or a content inventory can be a great source to start from. Your list will probably be too long, but try to generate a complete list initially.

145

For each card sort, aim to use about 50 of the most relevant cards. Keep track of the cards you don't use initially, because you may be able to introduce them later when you focus your research on specific categories. Having 40 cards ensures you'll generate the data you need to make decisions about your IA. Beyond 60 cards, participants will be less likely to complete your card sort. When you have a larger number of cards, you'll only be able to include the most relevant cards in any one card sort, but keep track of all cards, because you may use some discarded sets later, when you focus on subcategories within the main categories.

Recruiting Participants

For online, unmoderated testing, you can find or call for participants by using lists of customers, members, subscribers, or social media. You can also use an agency to recruit participants.

You can use a screener questionnaire to help you gather data from participants who have the attributes you want.

Tips for Card Sorting

If you're facing resource constraints, instead of starting with an open card sort, you may be tempted to start with a closed card sort and use categories based on assumptions or on an existing site. This may be appropriate when you are adding to an existing IA or if you have reason to believe that the IA will perform well.

It's acceptable to choose representative cards and then to assume that similar cards or tasks will perform similarly. Don't test edge cases unless those are the focus of your research.

When wording cards, use synonyms rather than priming participants with wording from the category or from other cards. Matching words will lead participants to specific choices and give misleading results.

Be sure to randomize the order in which participants see the cards and the categories—unless there's a specific order you must test. This removes list-primacy bias from the overall result.

Testing the Wording of Cards and Categories

Vary the wording of similar cards so participants don't simply group all cards that have the same terms. If you're providing categories, ensure they are clear and purposeful. It's a good idea to pre-test your study with your colleagues or a few initial participants. Attend the pre-test yourself to observe and probe the pre-testers' choices and interpretations. Then rewrite anything that is unclear. For a closed or hybrid card sort, you can also test for category names.

Analyzing and Interpreting the Data

The analysis and the interpretation of the data will depend on the type of card-sorting results (closed or open).

Interpreting Closed Card-Sorting Results

A closed card sort's category is predefined, so your research tool will show the frequency each card is sorted into each category. Most cards will map to one category, but some cards will map to multiple categories. You need to decide what to do with the ones that don't map clearly.

Example: A Closed Card Sort to Interpret

Figure 6-11 shows data from a card sort for a company's intranet. Most participants sorted the cards "Performance appraisal manual for all staff" and "Manual for managing employees" into the Employment category, but a minority of participants sorted these cards into "Day-to-day work and tools." The participant demographics (collected in a post-sort survey for this purpose) showed that most managers sorted these cards into day-to-day tasks because managing staff is part of their day-to-day work. This tells us to identify the intended reader in the IA's labeling and also in the introductions of these pages and to index the pages well for the site's search engine.

Interpreting Open Card-Sorting Results

An open card sort shows possible categories, as well as the frequency each card is sorted into each category. Most cards will map to one category, but some cards will map to multiple categories. You need to decide what to do with the ones that don't map

147

clearly. You also need to decide how to name the categories by analyzing the names that participants gave to them.

Cards	Day-to-day work and tools	Employment	Our purpose
Computer access while working remotely	94%	4%	2%
Meeting room sizes and locations	94%	2%	4%
Staff directory and organizational chart	93%	0%	7%
Security	76%	5%	19%
Building access for staff and guests	73%	9%	18%
Job opportunities	2%	96%	2%
Training & development	8%	92%	0%
Attendance and leave	15%	83%	2%
Performance appraisal manual for all staff	36%	62%	2%
Manual for managing employees	41%	57%	2%
Our vision and purpose	2%	3%	95%
Our executive	6%	0%	94%
Organizational structure (the "org chart")	19%	0%	81%
Press releases	23%	0%	77%
Communications	25%	2%	73%

Figure 6-11. *This is an excerpt of a much larger popular placements matrix generated by Optimal Workshop's OptimalSort. Due to rounding, some rows don't total 100 percent*

Start with a dendrogram to see the possible categories. Then use a similarity matrix to identify alternatives for parts of the dendrogram that don't seem to fit. Your software tool likely generates the dendrogram and matrix.

Example: An Open Card Sort to Interpret

Figure 6-12 shows an open card sort for a service design how-to site. In a dendrogram, the participants' combined results are sorted into three categories. You can see that one category is about team building and work principles, another is about how to conduct research, and a third is about analyzing and reporting research results.

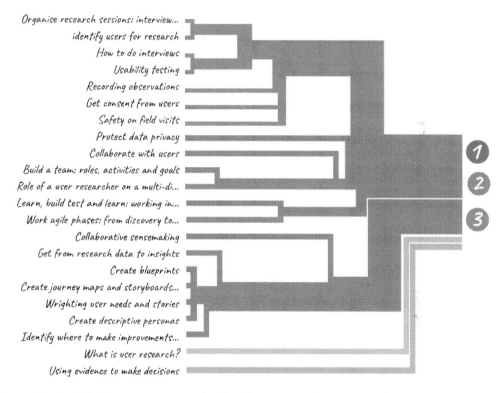

Figure 6-12. *This is an excerpt of a dendrogram, showing only 22 of the 40 cards that participants sorted. The researcher numbered the three branches*

Two cards didn't fit into the dendrogram categories. To find these cards a place, I used the similarity matrix generated from the same card-sorting data. The similarity matrix shows "What is user research?" and its relationship to all the other cards. Its highest scores show it is more closely related to cards from category 2 on the dendrogram. Similarly, I placed "Using evidence to make decisions" in category 3. See Figure 6-13.

Create blueprint

Label	1	2	3	4	5	6	7	8	9	10	11	12	13	14	15	16	17	18	19	20
Create journey maps and storyboards from research data	92																			
Create descriptive personas	65	96																		
Writing user needs and stories	93	97	94																	
Get from research data to insights	90	94	95	95																
Identify where to make improvements: pain points and happy paths	97	98	98	92	92															
Collaborative sensemaking	62	70	67	69	68	68														
Using evidence to make decisions	48	45	51	42	41	52	55													
Work in agile phases: from discovery to live	5	3	4	5	4	2	18	43												
Learn, build, test and learn work in an agile way	6	2	8	2	2	1	3	16	83											
Build a team: roles, activities and goals	2	0	2	5	2	6	2	19	61	68										
Role of a user researcher on a multi-disciplinary team	4	4	5	6	5	4	3	41	33	54	89									
Organise research sessions: interviews, observations, pop-up research	5	5	6	6	5	4	9	1	5	12	29	26								
What is user research?	0	4	1	8	4	8	14	42	31	52	75	84	62							
Protect data privacy	5	4	4	6	5	5	3	2	7	8	12	19	15	40						
Collaborate with users	6	5	4	1	5	2	12	43	45	33	33	15	45	65	95					
Get consent from users	4	5	3	1	3	2	13	33	16	18	17	7	69	35	28	31				
How to do interviews	4	2	4	5	1	3	12	16	4	4	8	4	80	44	11	17	83			
Recording observations	1	4	10	1	4	2	14	43	5	3	5	5	77	50	13	16	90	94		
Identify users for research	0	5	5	0	1	3	10	3	8	5	4	4	83	65	16	43	65	91	83	
Safety on field visits	4	1	5	4	5	1	9	6	9	12	7	9	82	48	36	54	83	70	67	83
Usability testing	3	6	3	4	11	15	11	44	14	16	17	20	95	33	12	18	62	83	83	68	72

Figure 6-13. *Table card sorting*

During an open card sort, participants enter labels for the groups they create. The researcher considers these and then chooses labels that best describe the categories, as shown in Figure 6-14.

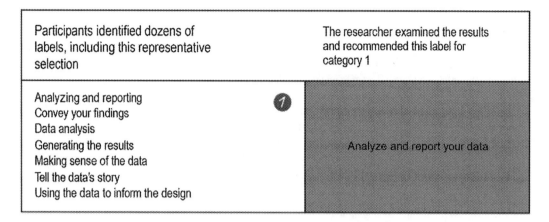

Figure 6-14. *Card sorting overview*

Presenting: What to Include in a Card Sorting Research Report

A typical report includes standard sections, such as an executive summary, your recommendations in summary and in full, a discussion, your research method, and supporting material. In the appendixes, include anything you think will help a nonspecialist reader to understand your report. Include the raw data in a spreadsheet.

Card Sorting Conclusion

Card sorting is a good method to help you to organize the information architecture of your site or product. One card sort may not be enough, and you should be ready to conduct several card sorts with different user groups. This of course makes it more complicated to analyze. It is also important to understand that users prefer using search functionality rather than going through the navigation to find information.

Summary

The most frequently quantitative research methods used to collect data in user research are analytics, surveying, and card sorting. These three approaches are used for specific purposes.

- Analytics is to understand what is going on your website and answer the questions how many, when, and which pages.

- Surveying is a great tool to validate qualitative findings with a larger sample size.

- Card sorting is a useful method if you want to rethink your information architecture and the navigation.

Alone, the quantitative research method in user research will not provide enough information to understand how users are using your product. While analytics could be used to keep an eye on the traffic and the activity of your website, surveys will validate questions that you already have, without leaving any room for unexpected avenues. Card sorting can also be a great approach to understand how users classify and group categories. Nevertheless, quantitative approaches used in isolation will provide only validation of preconceived ideas. I highly recommend using quantitative research approaches in association with qualitative research methods.

CHAPTER 7

Collecting Qualitative Data

Doing user research is also often associated with qualitative approaches, such as fieldwork and user testing. It is the core approach that we use in product development. Many people think that taking a qualitative approach is a smooth ride, or that everyone can do it. From my experience, a qualitative approach is not as easy as it seems: it is time-consuming, it takes years to master the research methods, and we have to continually fight for people to take the results seriously.

Honestly, when qualitative research is done correctly, the results are far more reliable and bring many more insights than some surveys. I never dismiss the quantitative approach, but both approaches should be used accordingly depending on the research questions. They are, in my opinion, complementary.

A qualitative approach requires a small sample. The analysis of the data is time-consuming and needs to be done methodically. In a way, the researcher will have to dive more deeply into the data to see what is going on.

It is essential to differentiate the methods that we use to collect data from the methods that we use to analyze data. Many UXers think that user research is just collecting data and using some sticky notes for the analysis phase. A proper analysis is often dismissed or forgotten.

Analyzing qualitative data takes more time than the data collection itself. Furthermore, it is essential to realize that there are as many methods to collect qualitative data as to analyze it. The methods that we can use to analyze qualitative data are grounded theory, discourse analysis, conversation analysis, ethnomethodology, thematic analysis, content analysis, etc. The method that we use the most in user research tends to be thematic analysis, which will be discussed in Chapter 8.

This chapter will look at the methods that we use to collect data, particularly contextual inquiries/ethnography, interviews, focus groups, user testing, and diary studies. This chapter will give you details on how to collect your data step-by-step.

© Emmanuelle Savarit 2020
E. Savarit, *Practical User Research*, https://doi.org/10.1007/978-1-4842-5596-4_7

Contextual Inquiry/Ethnography

Contextual inquiry is a qualitative research approach in which the researcher conducts a face-to-face semistructured/conversational interview within a user's natural environment (Figure 7-1). For example, if you want to build a new intranet, you have to spend time at the desk of the employees. If traders use your product, you have to spend time on the trading floor. If you are building a teaching tool, you have to spend time in the classroom.

Figure 7-1. *Home visit contextual inquiry*

The contextual inquiry aims at understanding the users and their needs before developing a new product. A contextual inquiry is an observational approach; the researcher looks at all the aspects of the environment.

It also permits researchers to capture personal information about the user. The contextual inquiry could be made in the home environment as well as in the workplace.

The researcher conducts fieldwork to capture data on how the users are using and interacting with a product in their natural environment. This approach provides valuable insight that would be missed in a lab or unfamiliar environment.

Additional advantages of this approach include the following:

- Having access to the real/natural environment

- Understanding the user in-situ

- Participants being more comfortable in their natural environment

- Being able to capture personal information about the user

- Enabling the research to identify unpredictable avenues

Disadvantages of this approach include the following:

- Time-consuming

- More challenging to record (generally we take notes and pictures)

- A bit intrusive

The fields of anthropology and ethnography influence contextual inquiry; anthropology is the study of human, language, culture, society, and human behavior, while ethnography is a scientific method that uses a systematic approach to study people and their culture.

> *"Ethnography is a type of qualitative research that gathers observations, interviews and documentary data to produce detailed and comprehensive accounts of different social phenomena." (Reeves et al., 2013)*

Many anthropologists have used and still use observation as a way of understanding people.

Contextual inquiry is sometimes described as a semistructured interview that investigates the context in the subject's environment. Contextual inquiry in user research is the way to enter the user's natural environment to understand how they behave, which tools they use, and how and when they interact with them. In user research, spending time in the user's natural environment allows us to understand the context and the user surroundings to see how they interact with their objects or any digital products. This helps us to clarify user needs and provide enlightenment on what we need to build to meet their needs.

When Using Contextual Inquiry

It is highly recommended to use contextual inquiry at the beginning of every project. During the discovery phase, contextual inquiry helps researchers to identify who the users are and what their needs are, as well as how your product is fitting into their environment, whether at home, at work, etc. It allows users to identify the current user journey, online and offline.

The naturally occurring data provides you with information that you wouldn't be able to capture otherwise. Findings from contextual inquiries give a better understanding of your users.

For example, in the workplace, observing a trader at his desk allows us to identify how many screens they use and which tools, software, and data they need to do their work. Understanding their day and which tasks they have to complete at different times helps us understand which information they will require at time t, etc. By sitting next to the user and observing their real day, you, as a researcher, can capture so much information that you will not be able to capture in a lab or while doing remote interviews or testing.

Conducting contextual inquiry as early as possible is a real advantage; you can also bring early prototypes or build a product and put it in front of the users. This means making the users use the product in their own setting.

Process to Conduct a Contextual Inquiry

Like any research project, you have to follow the same steps, as shown in Figure 7-2 and described in the following list.

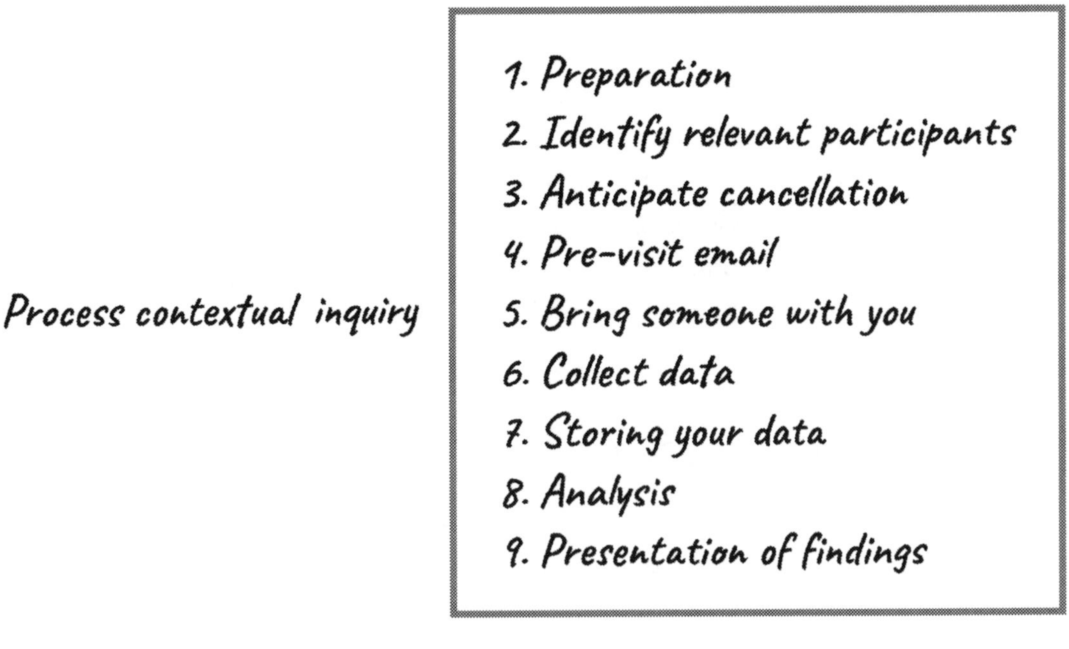

Process contextual inquiry

1. Preparation
2. Identify relevant participants
3. Anticipate cancellation
4. Pre-visit email
5. Bring someone with you
6. Collect data
7. Storing your data
8. Analysis
9. Presentation of findings

Figure 7-2. *Process contextual inquiry*

Preparing Your Contextual Inquiry

Here are some tips as you begin your project:

- Draw an account of what you want to find out.

- Prepare a discussion guide. Some people call it a script; this is a document in which you have the high-level questions/points that you want to cover during the session.

- When planning your schedule, allow enough time, as fieldwork visits always take much longer than lab sessions. You may have to travel, you may have some delays, the participants may be busy and you have to wait for them to be available.

- Regarding material preparation, how are you going to record the interaction? Are you going to use a video camera? Are you going to record the audio? Will you take some pictures? Verify that you have enough battery and also that you have a pen and a notebook in case you are not be able to record for some reason.

Identifying Relevant Participants

Identify the users you want to take part in your contextual inquiry. Recruit participants and prepare a screener (see Chapter 9 for details).

SMALL BUSINESS

One time I was conducting fieldwork to capture some information about a small business that hires apprentices. I went to a hair salon, a tailor shop, and even a large organization. When you go to a workplace, they may have other priorities, and you have to be patient and wait until they are available to talk to you. It's the same with a surgeon or medical consultant; I have spent hours in hospital corridors waiting for a consultant to have some free time.

Anticipating Cancellation

If you are doing a home visit, you have to understand that participants may cancel if they have something else coming up. Some people may also be intimidated and cancel at the last minute.

On the day of the visit, send another message to the participants to make sure they are still available. I've seen researchers travel across the country (in the United Kingdom) to collect data, and when they arrived, the participants were not available anymore. What a waste of time!

Sending a Pre-visit Email

Sending an email to the participants with the brief and a confirmation of the time of the visit is important. I recommend sending the consent form as well and asking them to send it back. You should by then know if you can record the session.

Bringing Someone with You

If you are doing a home visit, I recommend bringing someone with you for safety reasons. You can tell the participant that an assistant may attend the session too. It could be anyone from your team. Make sure they are doing something, such as helping you with the equipment but also taking notes. If you are going to an organization or a school, you won't need someone with you, but if you have someone who wants to see what it is like to make a contextual inquiry, ask them to take notes, which is always useful.

Collecting Your Data

When you arrive at the location for your data collection, you should start by introducing yourself.

Make sure you take the time to explain what you are going to do, what the format of the session is, and make sure that participants are comfortable with you taking pictures, recording, or even being in their home/workplace. If they are not comfortable, you should stop the interview (see Chapter 9).

Some people take notes with their computer, others on a notebook. This is, of course, a question of preferences, but sometimes it is essential to see how the note taking on the computer may affect the participant. Some people make more noise than others when typing.

For example, if your participant is a person of a certain age and you are doing a home visit, I recommend not being too intrusive. A computer may be intimidating for them, while it is not going to be intrusive in an open-plan office that is full of desktops and computers everywhere.

Knowing that user researchers are always running after time, taking notes on a computer may save time later. If it is possible, try to record the interaction with either audio or video. This way, it is easier to interact with the participant and have a normal conversation. They generally forget about the recording after a couple of minutes. Always ask if you can take pictures.

Try to keep having a natural conversation with your participants and not just read your script. You want to find out what you don't know, so be curious and ask a subsequent question if the participant starts saying something interesting. Ask them to show you which software they are using and how they are using it. What is working well and not well for them? Collecting the data in a natural environment is so rich. So many things are happening that it is essential to be open and curious, but we should not forget to capture what we plan to capture as well.

Use the following tools to collect the interview data:

- Dictaphone

- Computer

- Notebook and pen

- Camera

- Smartphone (audio recording, video, pictures)

Storing Your Data

Once the session is over, how you store it will depend on which type of data you have: notes, audio, video, screen captures, or pictures. Label and sort them into folders. If you have the time, recap your notes while they are still fresh in your mind. Having a recording is even better, as you can go back to your data at a later stage. Always have a backup for your data (external hard drive, on the cloud, and on your device). Nothing is worse than losing data after having done a session. Often when you lose data, it is always from an amazing participant.

Analysis

See Chapter 8 for more information about how to analyze qualitative data. The analysis is similar whether it's an interview, contextual inquiry, focus group, diary study, or user testing.

Presenting the Findings

You can find details on how to present the findings in Chapter 8.

Interviews

User interviews are frequently used to capture general information about users (Figure 7-3). There are three types of interviews: structured, semistructured, and unstructured.

Figure 7-3. Interview

Structured Interviews

A *structured interview* is the most controlled interview; it has a predefined response in which the participant can answer. Here is an example:

Which types of devices do you own?

- Smartphone
- Tablet
- Laptop
- Desktop
- Smart TV
- Smart speaker
- None of the above

How often do you watch streaming video?

- Several times a day
- Every day
- Several times a week
- Once a week
- Less than once a week
- Never

The structured interview may be quicker to analyze, but you may miss out on some unpredicted information.

Unstructured Interviews

An *unstructured interview* is the less controlled interview type; based on a natural conversation, the researcher has some general goal and topics that they want to cover. It's based on open-ended questions; then after the conversation gets going, the participant can answer with narrative and storytelling. It may be a bit challenging sometimes to stay on topic, but the data collected is very rich and generally provides some fantastic insight. It also allows the researcher to dig even more into the conversation. The researcher/moderator must get the participant back on track when it is needed. Some participants have difficulties stopping once they get going.

Semistructured Interviews

The *semistructured interview* is the combination of both structured and unstructured; it starts with structured questions such as demographics, general information, and specific technology subjects. The structured interview questions at the beginning also help to warm up the participant; these are followed by open-ended questions. This is a good option that provides some straightforward data as well as some valuable data.

Preparation of Your Interview Questions

The interview questions need to be well-written, clear, and concise; not leading; and use terminology that is easy to understand.

Test your questions with your team and stakeholders. If you are not sure about your questions, do not hesitate to ask someone. It is always good to have someone else to look at them. It is also recommended that you do a pilot run through your questionnaire with someone before you start interviewing participants.

Interview Format

The format is generally the same whichever interview format you are using.

1. Researcher's introduction, explanation of the format of the interview, ethical issues (anonymous, right to withdraw at any time; see Chapter 7), confirmation of consent if it is face-to-face

2. Warm-up questions

3. Questions

4. Recap

5. Wrap-up, thank you, etc.

Different Ways to Conduct Interviews

There are several ways to conduct interviews, such as a face-to-face interviews, phone interviews, and remote video interviews.

- **Telephone:** The telephone is impersonal, and you cannot see the face or behavior of your participant when they answer the questions. It is still possible to record the phone interview, which I recommend. A telephone interview needs to be short, as it is difficult to get participants fully engaged after 15 to 20 minutes.

- **Face-to-face:** The advantage of the face-to-face interview is that you can get a proper social interaction that provides nonverbal communication as well as verbal communication. The researchers get more information through the interview, and the data should be more fruitful. The sessions can be audio and video recorded. You can do it at any location, but it may be time-consuming for the participant and the researcher, especially if anyone has to travel to get there.

- **Remote interviews:** This area is growing recently with the improvement of video conferencing. More and more meetings occur through video conferencing. It is easier to organize, and it is possible to record the data audio or video depending on the participant consent. You still get the nonverbal communication (not as natural as face-to-face), but it is an excellent way to collect data.

- **Online chat:** It is becoming more frequent to use chat to ask questions. Generally there should be a maximum five questions to make sure participant reply to the questions after the user drops out. Here you can only use close-ended questions.

Using Interviews to Collect Data

With qualitative methods, you are most likely to use an interview at some point. If you are making a contextual inquiry, you should start with some interview questions. With a user testing session, you can also start with some general interview questions to warm up your participants. Also, it is common to combine interviews with user testing. It's the same with a diary study; you have to do the first visit at the beginning of a diary study and also at the end for the post-diary interview.

You'll need to identify relevant participants (a section in Chapter 9 is dedicated to how to recruit the relevant participants).

Anticipate cancellation if you are doing interviews; participants may decide to cancel the session if they have something else coming up. Some people may also be intimidated and cancel at the last minute. If you are using a recruitment agency to bring participants to a specific location, I would make sure that they have some backup participants, and they should make sure that the participants are showing up.

If you are managing the recruitment yourself, I recommend providing all the information to the participants well in advance. The day before, you can send a text message or event to call the participant to make sure they are still on board. I also suggest sending another message on the day of the interview.

Use the following tools to collect the interview data:

- Dictaphone

- Computer

- Notebook and pen

- Camera

- Smartphone (audio recording, video, pictures)

- Video conference tool that records audio and video

- Phone app to record the conversation

Storing Your Data

Make sure all your data is in one place. You have to organize the data as some of it may be notes, video, or audio. You have to make sure that you centralize the data and transcribe it to be in the same format to analyze it. Analyzing the data and presenting the findings are both discussed in Chapter 8.

Focus Groups

A focus group is a session that lasts between one and two hours and takes place with six to ten participants who discuss a specific topic (see Figure 7-4). Focus groups have been used a lot in marketing to understand a point of view or trend or to test a new product. The focus group session could happen in a room with a one-way mirror, even if that is a bit intimidating for the participants. It is also possible to run a focus group in a meeting room and set up small cameras around the room to record the session. It is also possible to project the session in another room.

Figure 7-4. *Focus group*

What is interesting about a focus group is the energetic level of discussion that may be able to bring up some new topics.

The role of the moderator is crucial, so they need some moderation skills, as it is complex to manage all the participants at the same time. It is important to make sure all the participants can express their opinions. The researcher should make sure that it is not always the same participant who is taking the lead on every topic. You don't want to forget the more introverted/quieter participants. During a focus group session some new topics may arise, and the researcher has to control them, especially if you run a focus group with ten participants, which can easily get off-topic.

When to Use Focus Groups in User Research

It is difficult to test a product with a group; you can show a demo and see the user's first impression. If you want to find out what your client's issues are, I recommend conducting a focus group with the operators of your call center; they are on the front line, speaking every day with your customers and clients. They can help you identify some issues instead of doing interviews with your clients.

Focus groups could be useful when you want your stakeholders involved in the project. Stakeholders can give their opinions and discuss the topic. You could also make the stakeholder focus group mode interactive and make them use some sticky notes.

Preparing Your Interview Questions

The questions of the focus group should be semistructured and open. You can't have too many questions as you need all the participants to participate. It is recommended to pin down three to four topics to help you to answer your research questions. Avoid delicate topics, and make sure your questions are clear.

Format of Focus Groups

There is a process to follow to moderate a focus group session.

1. Moderator introduction

2. Participants introduction

3. Warm-up questions about the topics (general)

4. Topics (depends on how many topics you want to cover)

5. Wrap-up

6. Conclusion/debrief

Collecting the Data

So much is going on during a focus group that it is challenging to take notes. It is highly recommended to record the sessions and also to have people in the viewing room to take notes at the same time. The note-taking should happen in the viewing room to extract the main points that the participants are making. If the participants are internal staff, you may be able to have the note-taker in the same room.

Materials

Here are the materials that you need to conduct a focus group:

- Video cameras.

- Notebook.

- Discussion guide.

- Consent forms.

- Lab with one-way mirrors. (This can be disturbing for the participants; having a separate room with a projection may be better for them.) I find that some isolation between the viewing room with a one-way mirror can be a bit noisy and disturbs not only the participant but also the researcher.

- One meeting room with the focus group and another one with the projection of the recordings.

Storing the Data

Make sure all your data is in one place; you have to organize it as it may be in different forms such as notes, video, and audio. You have to make sure that you centralize the data and transcribe it to be all on the same format to analyze it.

Analysis and Presentation of the Findings

You can find details on how to analyze qualitative data as well as how to present the findings in Chapter 8.

Usability Testing/User Testing

Usability testing/user testing is a face-to-face session with real users who are interacting with the product not only to evaluate the functionalities and the efficiency but also to capture the user's behavior, motivation, and frustration in a situation (Figure 7-5).

Figure 7-5. *Remote user testing*

Initially, usability tests concentrated on how efficient, effective, and usable a product was, based on success or failure or task completion and the time it took a participant to perform and complete the task. What we mean by usability testing is testing that occurs in a controlled environment, often in a lab. We could associate it with experimental research design. Usability testing aims to improve the platform/interface by testing the user journey and identifying any blockers that may interfere with the flaws of performing the tasks.

The discipline has matured over the years. In the last few years, the discipline took a more natural, organic approach that goes beyond performance. What is now important is the integration of the product into the user's life and environment. Furthermore, what are the user's motivations to use your product? The term *usability* is used a lot with different definitions, from automated testing for accessibility to sessions in a lab environment. I differentiate usability from user testing.

Usability, based on its origin, is associated with quantifying success rate, task on time, error rates, and satisfaction. You can think of user testing as an observational approach to evaluate how users interact with the product, what their motivation is to use it, and how it fits into their natural environment, life, and context.

I use the term *user testing*, instead of usability testing. I find that user testing takes a broader approach that includes usability, A/B testing, lab user testing, remote user testing, guerrilla/pop-up testing, natural environment testing, and eye-tracking.

Advantages of this approach include the following:

- Able to catch any issues in terms of design, functionalities, and content before launching a product

- Able to test a new concept or prototype

- Able to see how the user may interact with the product

- Able to test the end-to-end user journey

- Able to save time in the product development

- Able to help understand the users

- Able to provide an objective evaluation of your product

Disadvantages may include the following:

- It can feel unnatural and experimental if done in a lab.

- It is time-consuming.

- It has a cost.

Usability Testing

In a usability testing session, you have the ability to use different approaches, listed here:

- To compare different designs, you can do an A/B testing.

- To find out how people are navigating through the site, to test the content, or to evaluate if the user can see some of the features, you can use eye-tracking.

- To spend some time with employees or back-office staff or to spend time with users just to test some features or modifications, you can do guerrilla/pop-up research.

- To have a fast collaborative approach with the UX and design team, a RITE approach may be used.

- A lab testing versus natural environment will be decided depending on the time constraints, context, and objectives.

- Remote testing is a good compromise.

A/B Testing

A/B testing is the comparison of two or more versions when you want to test two designs, different content, placement of a button, different colors, etc. It is a quick way to get some external feedback instead of making the decision internally. You can integrate A/B testing into a general user testing session.

Eye-Tracking

Eye-tracking is a tool that captures the gaze of the user while using a product. You use eye-tracking during a user testing session. Most of the time eye-tracking is done on a desktop or laptop. Eye-tracking technology has improved; now you can have some gaze capturing that is not intrusive and is portable, with a smooth eye calibration. I recommend using eye-tracking when you want to test a product that includes a lot of information. The eye-tracking data provides valuable information for analysis, such as where the user is looking at. I find that eye tracking is perfect for testing navigation and also content. As well as capturing the gaze, the software can capture the screen, mouse, audio, and video of the session. Many people like heat maps, which are helpful to add to your report presentation. Personally, I find that the new Tobii eye-tracking software now called Tobii Pro is amazing and facilitates the analysis.

Guerrilla Testing/Pop-Up Research

Guerrilla testing is a quick user testing session in which the researcher puts a design in front of the user. It can be as quick as 15 to 20 minutes. You can also record the session and do it from your laptop. You can use this method as soon as possible; I recommend during alpha.

RITE

Rapid Interactive Testing and Evaluation (RITE) is a method to work on fast alterations on a prototype. This method alternates over one or several weeks. The RITE process is based on alternating one day of testing with one-day design updates, another day of testing, and so on.

Using RITE is good when you work on a spike, something you want to create quickly using a co-constructing design between the designer, users, and researcher.

Lab vs. Natural Environment

There are many points of views regarding collecting data in a lab or the user's natural environment.

It is quite challenging to get people to come to a lab. I realize that sometimes participants are more willing to take part in research if it takes place at their workplace, at home, or in a convenient location nearby. Now with the improvement of software to capture data, it is not necessary to go to a lab to access the material for the data collection. Still, lab testing can be quite powerful if you want to have a member of your team to watch the sessions. Also, if you want to get the stakeholder to get involved in your project, lab sessions are good for that. From a participant's point of view, lab testing tends to be a bit experimental, which denotes what would happen in real life.

If you want to use a lab, the cost tends to be on average £1000 ($1240 USD) per day.

Remote Testing

It is not always possible to travel to the user's location or to make the user travel to a lab, especially when you want to have a diversified sample. Doing user testing in a single location is risky and leads to sample bias.

It is recommended that you conduct remote testing sessions. Today, it is easier to conduct remote testing sessions. We have access to reliable software that allows us to capture data remotely through a video communication tool. There are many tools now such as Zoom, GoToMeeting, WebEx, and Hangouts. I like using Zoom, since it allows you to share the screen and record the session. Remote testing is used often while conducting international research. Conducting international research with China is more complicated. You need to be a bit creative as many of the software are blocked. You may use WeChat or, if they are using Microsoft Teams, ask them to share their screen. You can add QuickTime in the back to record the screen.

System Usability Scale

The System Usability Scale (SUS) was created by John Brooke in 1986. It is a quick usability test that is now a UX standard. It helps to evaluate software, hardware, mobile devices, websites, apps, etc.

SUS could be in the quantitative chapter, but I tend to do it at the end of user testing sessions; therefore, I put it in this chapter.

The SUS provides a high-level satisfaction score of the usability of a site, application, or any technological item. SUS is a simple, ten-item scale giving a global view of subjective assessments of usability.

The SUS (Figure 7-6) is used after the respondent has had an opportunity to use the system/product. I ask participants to complete it before any debriefing or discussion takes place.

SUS scores have a range of 0 to 100. It is not a percentage. A score above 68 is above average, and a score below 68 is below average.

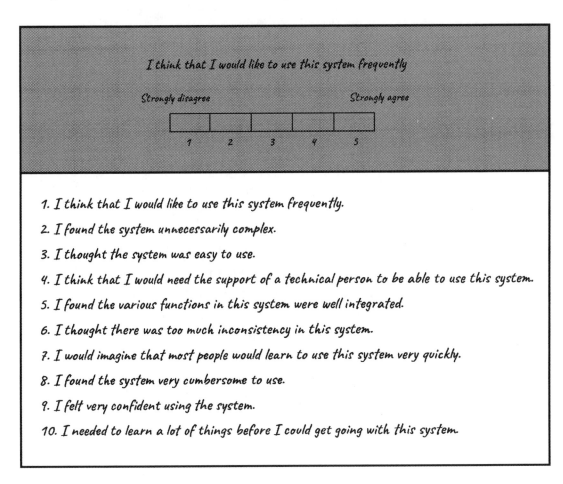

I think that I would like to use this system frequently

Strongly disagree   Strongly agree

1   2   3   4   5

1. I think that I would like to use this system frequently.

2. I found the system unnecessarily complex.

3. I thought the system was easy to use.

4. I think that I would need the support of a technical person to be able to use this system.

5. I found the various functions in this system were well integrated.

6. I thought there was too much inconsistency in this system.

7. I would imagine that most people would learn to use this system very quickly.

8. I found the system very cumbersome to use.

9. I felt very confident using the system.

10. I needed to learn a lot of things before I could get going with this system.

Figure 7-6. SUS questionnaire

Calculating SUS Score

The following steps detail how to calculate manually the System Usability Scale score:

1. Sum the score contributions from each item.

2. Each item's score contribution will range from 0 to 4. For items 1, 3, 5, 7, and 9, the score contribution is the scale position minus 1.

3. For items 2, 4, 6, 8, and 10, the contribution is 5 minus the scale position. Multiply the sum of the scores by 2.5 to obtain the overall SUS value.

4. Once you have all your participants' individual scores, then you total the sum and divide it by the number of participants. You then get the overall score (Figure 7-7).

Formula for SUS Excel Calculation

Here's the formula to add to your Excel spreadsheet:

```
Copy and change the row number
```

```
=((B4-1)+(5-C4)+(D4-1)+(5-E4)+(F4-1)+(5-G4)+(H4-1)+(5-I4)+(J4-1)+(5-K4))*2.5
=((B5-1)+(5-C5)+(D5-1)+(5-E5)+(F5-1)+(5-G5)+(H5-1)+(5-I5)+(J5-1)+(5-K5))*2.5
```

L4			fx	=((B4-1)+(5-C4)+(D4-1)+(5-E4)+(F4-1)+(5-G4)+(H4-1)+(5-I4)+(J4-1)+(5-K4))*2.5							
	A	B	C	D	E	F	G	H	I	J	K	L
1	SUS Calculation											
2												
3	Participant	q1	q2	q3	q4	q5	q6	q7	q8	q9	q10	SUS Score
4	p1	3	4	2	2	2	3	2	3	3	4	40.0
5	p2	5	2	4	1	3	2	4	2	4	1	80.0
6	p3	5	2	4	1	4	1	5	1	5	1	92.5
7	p4											50.0
8	p5											50.0
9	p6											50.0
10	p7											50.0
11	p8											50.0

Figure 7-7. *SUS calculation*

Interpretation

The data interpretation depends on the stage you are at in your product development. I highly recommend using SUS after every user testing session to see the evolution of the score through your product development. The score should get better after the alterations. If the score is going down after making some changes, it may inform you that the alteration may not be the right one or that the added features are affecting the overall usability of your product (Figure 7-8).

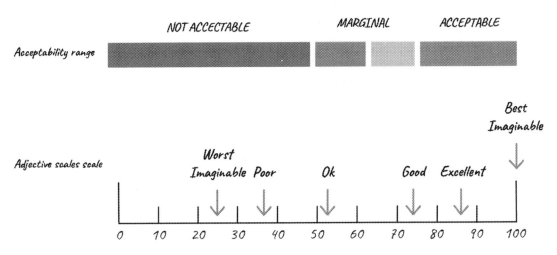

Figure 7-8. *SUS interpretation*

When to Do User Testing?

User testing needs to be incorporated into the product development as soon as you have some screens. If you already have a live product, the method to collect data may depend on the product development phase you are in.

- **Alpha**: RITE, pop-up research, and remote testing.

- **Beta**: Pop-up research, user testing in natural and in lab, with or without eye tracking, as well as remote testing.

- **Live**: End-to-end user testing sessions, walk-through, with or without eye-tracking. It could be done in a natural environment, in a lab, or remotely.

To do usability testing to evaluate the effectiveness of a product, the product needs to be live or in private beta. You need to have real data to enable participants to use the product and go through the user journey. You can't evaluate the effectiveness and time on tasks on a prototype.

I recommend doing user testing if you want to evaluate the end-to-end user journey, especially while launching your new website. You can also test the end-to-end journey on your current site to evaluate its usability and any issues that could block the user journeys.

Preparation of Your User Testing Sessions

This section will describe the different steps that are involve in preparing you user testing session.

Plan

Prepare a research plan with the primary goal of the user testing, and also state what is out of scope. You won't be able to test everything. Therefore, you have to create a clear statement of what you are going to test. It is essential for you, your team, and your stakeholders.

Materials

Get your materials ready. Once you have the prototypes or the screens, or live product, you should prepare your discussion guide.

The discussion guide should include the following:

- A brief introduction to the research.

- An overview of the testing.

- The warm-up questions that generally are related to demographics, technology usage, and general questions about the topic. For example, if you are testing a travel website or app, the questions about the topic will be related to how often they travel, which transportation they use, and how they book their travel.

- The heart of the testing should be on the screens you want to get feedback. If the participants understand what the screen is about, how is the navigation, the layout, the design, the terminology, and so on? You may include A/B testing or some tasks.

- Wrap-up is to reiterate what the user had said.

- Conclusion to thank the participant.

The Consent Form

You have to ask participants for their consent (see Chapter 9).

Equipment

Make sure your equipment is set up in advance, such as laptops, smartphones, mobile devices, tablets, software to capture the data, any other equipment such as Apple TV to project the data in the room next door, etc. Test your equipment beforehand.

Participants' Recruitment and Schedule

Participant recruitment is discussed in Chapter 9. Make sure you have all the details about your participants and set a clear schedule.

Hardware Storage

You need to make sure you have enough storage on your laptop or use secure cloud storage.

Analysis of the Data and Presentation of the Findings

Like in previous methodologies, the analysis and the presentation of the data are discussed in Chapter 8.

Diary Study

Diary study is a qualitative research method (see Figure 7-9). This method to collect data comes from anthropology and ethnography.

Figure 7-9. *Diary study*

Around since the early 1900s, *ethnography* means using diary studies. These approaches aim to look at social phenomenon, rather than taking a quantitative experimental approach. A diary study is a document that a participant completes by recording events of their lives. In user research, the diary study also involves the usage of a device, product, software, etc.

This approach permits us to get insights from users while they are experiencing a situation. The study is longitudinal and captures temporal information.

Diary studies are used a lot in the field of education to understand the learning process. A longitudinal study involves student and teacher and also parents when it is about children learning methods or product usage. Diary studies are also commonly used in the fields of psychology, sociology, anthropology, medical, and historical research.

Now, diary studies are used often to capture insight during the development of a new digital product. Participants can self-report their behaviors, frustrations, opinions, desires, and aspirations at scheduled intervals or while asked to perform a task.

Advantages of this method include the following:

- To understand how people use a device, product, or service

- To answer why

- To give more insights

- To understand who your user is

- To identify new phenomena

It is a nonintrusive method of research; participants can log information when they are pleased, and it doesn't require a researcher observing.

Disadvantages include the following:

- Participants may not be proactive.

- Participants may not always be objective.

Using a Diary Study to Collect Data

It is recommended to use a diary study when a product is ready to go live. Diary studies permit us to capture what is happening in the user's everyday life. They provide valuable context for the interpretation of the data. They also indicate how the product is integrated into the participants' experiences.

Using a diary study is highly valuable when a participant uses the product repetitively (several times over the week), such as if you plan to see how participants are using a streaming service to watch movies or series.

While doing user testing sessions, you may miss out completely on how your product integrates into the participant's real life.

In the case of a streaming service, the user may be using the service several times a week. Or if the product is a speaker such as Alexa, how does it fit into people's homes? Where do they locate it? Or how is business-to-business software going to be integrated into the work environment?

Ideally, you could use a diary study when you are testing a prototype that is already functional (private beta). Diary studies help to see how the user is using a product over some time. They also help to see whether the participants develop any habits over the period. It enables researchers to get insight such as participants' impressions but also frustration that may appear over time.

Process to Conduct a Diary Study

As with the previous qualitative approaches, when you want to carry out a diary study, you have to do following:

- Identify what you want to find out.

- Who are your participants? How do you recruit them?

Standard screening procedures can be used to recruit participants: identify the use profile(s), create a screener survey, and distribute it through the appropriate channels (see the Chapter 9 Participants recruitment, ethics and accessibility).

- Plan how to collect the data. Which format would be the best to capture the data? Which tasks do you want to test?

    You should document all the preparation:

    - Prepare a discussion guide for the pre-meeting.

    - Draft the scenario for the task.

    - Plan how you are going to deliver the tasks (e.g., by sending an email or a message on the chat?). Provide several envelopes to the participants with the instructions inside. The envelopes could be opened at different times through the diary study.

    - You should also prepare a discussion guide for a post-diary interview.

    - You could also give a SUS.

- You'll have to choose the material that you want to use for a diary study.

    Diary studies initially used notebooks (paper diary) to capture what was going on. Now, we have digital tools (websites, apps, etc.) that enable the participants to collect the entries. Participants can make notes, take pictures, and make some video recordings. Diary studies are becoming more manageable now, with the democratization of the smartphone. You should keep in mind that participants need to have enough storage on their phone to collect the data. Furthermore, the researchers also need to make sure they have enough storage to store the data.

Tools to Collect the Interview Data

You can have a pre-meeting to introduce the research to the participant. You need to look at how participants can share the diary entries with you. Do you want them to complete a paper diary? Or to go digital?

A paper diary is a more traditional way to capture the information. You may miss out on the context, however. Also, you need to wait until the diary study is completed to access the data. They may also be handwritten, which may be challenging to read, and you need to transcribe them to analyze the paper diary.

If you go for the paper diary, make sure the participant has all the instructions in advance. You can use a face-to-face session to explain the study and what to expect from the participants. Also, give them a contact number. The data must be anonymized; therefore, you should ask the participant to use a number instead of a name on the notebook.

- Digital diary: You could also ask the participants to record their entries in a Word document and to send it to you regularly by email. Have a separate email for the reception of the documents and images. Once the researcher has received the documents, I recommend making the data anonymous. Create a folder, remove participants' names, and label the data with a number on all the documents.

- WhatsApp/WeChat/Messenger, etc.: Using chat is also an excellent way to collect data; it is less time-consuming for the participant, especially if they are using chat to communicate with their friends and families. Chat is an excellent way to collect data as you can monitor the entries and ask further questions based on what you have read and seen.

You can export the chat to a Word or text document and transfer the pictures and the video to a folder.

Some people use Google Docs or any cloud drive; this may be easier for the researcher, as the participant directly uploads the document in the right folder. It is a bit more time-consuming for the participant. The organization of the data is the same as the chat method once you create your folders.

Some tools are available on the market, such as Indeemo, which I find is excellent from a researcher's point of view. It has a dashboard but is too complicated for the participants to use.

Dscout seems very nice and is highly recommended by a digital anthropologist. Still, it is costly, with a minimum of $5,000 for an average project. It is already hard enough to get a budget for research.

I recommend using the same method for all the data entries, as using several different methods to collect may complicate the data management as well as the data analysis.

Once you have decided on the method to use, you can plan your diary study.

Collecting Your Data

Here are some points to take into consideration while you are collecting diary study data:

- I recommend conducting the pre-research meeting face to face. If it is not possible to be there physically, it is always possible to do it with a remote video conference tool (Skype, Zoom, Hangouts, etc.).

- Participants could be asked specific questions throughout the study, or they may have the freedom to express their experience through notes, pictures, or video recordings. The participants should follow the instructions based on your discussion guide.

- Moderation of the data entries is essential as you may identify something that you want to investigate further. You can also identify that the participant is not proactive and not uploading enough entries. Keeping an eye on the data can help you to flag it and contact the participant to help them upload the data. It is more complicated when it is a paper diary to monitor the data entries.

- An interview post diary is essential to get some retrospective of the overall experience, including the user's frustration level, how the product was doing, etc. It is also a good time to investigate any more interesting behavior that you have identified throughout the diary study.

Hardware Storage

You need to make sure you have enough storage on your laptop or use secure cloud storage.

Challenges

The quality of the data in a diary relies heavily on the participant commitment to provide data.

One challenge while conducting a diary study is to make sure the participants are proactive. It is not always easy to make a recording of their experience. Sometimes, we need to put in place some reminders or provide them with a schedule to submit their feedback on a regular basis.

I highly recommend giving a generous incentive to participants who are conducting a diary study. You should also acknowledge that it may be time-consuming for them to make all the diary entries (notes, pictures, video, etc.), and some researchers even give a nominal incentive per entry.

Analysis of the Data and Presentation of the Findings

Like for the other qualitative research methods described in this chapter, the analysis of qualitative data and how to present user research findings are covered in Chapter 8.

Summary

This chapter looked at contextual inquiries, interviews, focus groups, user testing, and diary studies as they are the main methods to collect qualitative data in user research. The researcher can pick and choose the most appropriate methods depending on the research questions or the development phase. The format of the data in qualitative research methods could be notes, audio, video, or screen recordings. Once your data is collected and organized, the analysis can start.

The next chapter will give you a step-by-step method of how to analyze your data using a thematic analysis.

CHAPTER 8

Analyzing Qualitative Data and Interpreting the Findings

After looking at the different methods to collect data in the previous chapter, we now have notes, audio, video, and screen captures to work with. This can be a considerable amount of data. Qualitative data is very rich when you start looking at it in detail, and content analysis is an excellent method to analyze data from contextual inquiries, interviews, focus groups, and user testing. In this chapter, we'll review several qualitative research methods that can be used to analyze user research data.

Affinity Diagrams

A fast way to analyze data is to create an affinity diagram. Jiro Kawakita created this method that simplifies a large amount of data by grouping it by the themes that emerge from the data. You generally use data from all the participants and write notes on cards or sticky notes. Then you group them. This analysis should be done with as much objectivity as possible. I recommend using an affinity diagram if you are observing interviews, focus groups, or user testing, or while running a workshop with stakeholders. During the session, the team can write comments on sticky notes and put them on the wall. At the end of the sessions, the team and the researchers can group the notes into categories. It is a great team exercise that brings everyone to the same level; there is no

© Emmanuelle Savarit 2020
E. Savarit, *Practical User Research*, https://doi.org/10.1007/978-1-4842-5596-4_8

place for preconceived ideas. The researcher needs to moderate the session and make sure the following affinity diagram rules are respected:

- Put your team in a room.

- Get some sharpies and sticky notes.

- Explain the rules of affinity diagrams.

- Create equality across the team. (Stakeholders are equal to everyone else on the team.)

- There are no preconceived ideas and no right or wrong ideas.

- All ideas are suitable for an affinity diagram exercise; some categorizations may merge or drift apart.

- A different team member may have the same category.

- Everyone in the team creates the cards and groups them on the wall.

- Label the groups.

- Look at duplicated groups and then regroup them.

- Organize your groups based on the amount of data in each group.

- Go through all the groups, labels, and descriptions with your team.

- Take a picture of your diagram.

This method is suitable for brainstorming or early-stage analysis to identify the different steps of a user journey.

The affinity diagram is also useful to develop a persona or to identify all the crucial steps of a user journey, especially if it involves several users going through online and offline paths.

Thematic Analysis vs. Content Analysis

Content analysis converts systematic patterns into code and then translates qualitative data into quantitative data. The researchers get into the qualitative data and start coding it; you need to have at least two researchers to code the data to compare the coding, and you have to recode the data until the researchers agree with the coding. They will then group the data under each code. Once they have organized the data into categories, the amount of input under each category can be compatibilized.

Thematic analysis relies on the same principles as content analysis, in a sense that we look at patterns and systematicity. The thematic analysis allows themes to emerge from the data but also looks at systematic themes that recur while doing user research. For example, when we are doing user testing sessions, we often look at the following themes:

- Navigation

- Design

- Layout

- Font

- Contrast

- Content

- Terminology

We can transcribe the quotes from each participant into an Excel document. We also look at the behaviors, the motivation of the participants, and their current habits. For example, say you want to find out how they book their flights. You can start identifying different behaviors for doing this. While doing a thematic analysis, we can start identifying systematic themes in the data in the same session but also across the participants. To analyze the data, it is important to start to compile it.

Compiling the Data

You have to put all your data together and organize it per participant. For example, you may have demographic information from your participants; you may also have information about their technology usage and the devices they own. You may also have videos, pictures, audio files, and notes. Make sure you label all your data, but do not use the name of the participant (for ethical reasons).

- Summarize your notes, using "participant 1," "participant 2," etc.

- Label all your documents.

- Organize your data in a single place. I put all the data in a folder, with a subfolder for every participant.

- Once all your data is stored in a centralized place, it is easier to start the analysis.

Going Back to the Data

Once all your data is organized in one single location, you can start by going back to it. Read your notes, look at the pictures, put them on the wall, and recall what happened. I highly recommend going back to the audio, video, and screen recordings. Put your headphones on, listen, and observe what is going on.

Transcription

Ideally, it is a good idea to transcribe first and then to analyze the transcript. The issue is that with a transcript, you get only the audio. If you are using video or even screen captures, you have to run a multimodal analysis, which involves speech, nonverbal communication, facial behaviors, gazes, and gestures, as well as all the activity on the screen. Doing this detail of transcription requires years of expertise in transcribing and requires you to be pragmatic. User researchers do not have enough time to do such detailed transcriptions.

I recommend using an Excel document. You can start by writing the main observations. This could be what the participants say or what they are doing. It could also be that the participant has managed to complete the tasks or that the participant could not see the button or couldn't understand the content.

All the important points should be recorded in the Excel document. To record all the important stuff, you have to go back to the data.

Excel Document/Analysis

The Excel document is part of your analysis. Not only can you record a snapshot of what is going on in your data, but you can record at what time it occurs. This helps you identify where a specific phenomenon occurs; you can go back to it and make a short clip. Data is very rich, and sometimes you may identify a theme that may not be relevant at this stage of the product development, but you still record it in your Excel document.

For example, we tested a specific task to try some new screens, but during the testing, we found that setting up a password was an issue. We created a theme of "password creation" and recorded what every user did, the number of attempts, comments, and where they were making the errors. Even though this was not the purpose of the user testing, several weeks later, the product owner said that they realized in the analytics that they had some issues with the creation of the password. The product owner wanted to do some user testing to understand what the issues were. We did not need to run another user testing because we already had the data and could extract the clips and rewatch the sessions. We could quickly summarize the findings, provide the evidence of where the issues were, and make some recommendations. Figure 8-1 shows the process to analyze data.

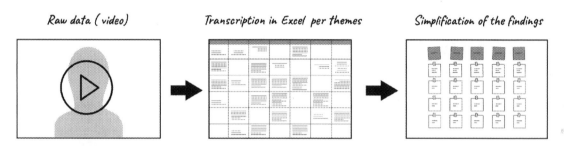

Figure 8-1. *Process to analyze data*

Identifying Systematic Phenomena Across the Data

In this section, let's say we are looking at a new app for booking a flight. We conducted ten user testing sessions. We had some general questions about how users book their flights and to find out their motivation. The best way to get a natural answer is for the user to tell a story or to recall their last flight booking. The project aims to understand the different types of users as well as test the user journey of booking a flight. We could identify the following:

- One category of users includes people who always look at a comparison website to get the best offer. Or they may look at a different site and make the comparison themselves (best offer).

- Another category of users includes loyal customers of a national airline because they are part of their loyalty program (loyal).

- Another category of users includes frequent flyers who travel a lot for work (business).

- Another category of users includes people who are adventurous and love traveling and are always looking for a deal (adventurous).

- You may identify a user who only looks for a flight based on the airport preference (commodity).

- You may also distinguish users who are price-driven from the ones who are more comfort-driven (comfort).

We can categorize and make a theme for every step through the user journey, such as the following:

- Landing page

- Selecting the city of departure

- Selecting the destination

- Selecting the departure date

- Selecting the return date

- Selecting the number of passengers

In each category, we can transcribe what the user is saying. What is the user doing? How is the user reacting to every page? Also, if you are using eye-tracking, where is the user looking? We can also get feedback on the themes that we already identified with previous participants.

If we identify that the user makes the same comments while booking a flight or conveys the same issues or frustration, that means we have identified a systematic pattern across the data. This is a new category, and we should make it a theme.

Extracting the Findings

Once you have completed your Excel document, you can go back to the content and summarize it with one keyword per the theme. Then you can group the themes by similarity. You will start seeing the main themes emerging from the analysis.

RECAP

---

1. Remember what the goal of your research was.

2. Review your research questions.

3. Go back to the data.

4. Transcribe the important comments, behaviors, issues, etc., that you have identified.

5. Create themes as you go through the data.

Once the data is in the Excel document, read all the inputs again and create a simplified list of themes of what is happening. Draw a list of all the themes that you have identified. Prioritize the themes based on systematicity across the session and across the participants.

The same process occurs for contextual inquiry. For example, when was testing a new service related to apprenticeship, I visited small businesses such as a hair salon, a beauty salon, tailors, jewelry shops, etc. We make some observations, took some notes, took some pictures, and recorded the audio of our conversations. Once we put the data together, we started going back to it, listing the main findings in an Excel.

Overview of the Findings

Once you have completed your analysis, I recommend preparing an overview of the findings on an A4 document. The document should present the main themes and subthemes that emerged from your data with some high-level comments. It is important to get this document ready as soon as possible to share it quickly with the rest of your team.

User Journey

The user journey represents the different steps that the user takes while performing a task or a series of actions to achieve something.

User Journey: Discovery

Before starting to build a new product (in discovery), it is essential to understand the current user journey. This could be online if you have a legacy product, or the user journey could be offline.

The objective is to identify the current user journey. Answer these questions:

- What are the different steps?

- Which actions need to be performed?

- How often is the user performing the tasks? This allows you to identify what can be simplified or replaced by some automation. Keep a list of all the screens that need to be created.

It also allows you to identify blockers, issues, and the complexity of the journey. See Figure 8-2.

EXAMPLE 1: USER JOURNEY RECRUITMENT

After organizing one or several workshops and discussing the process with the back-office team, we extracted all the steps that the team went through to recruit a new employee.

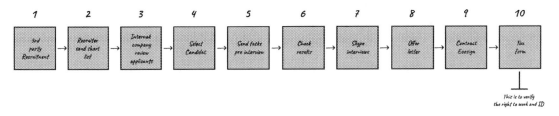

Figure 8-2. *User journey recruitment*

User Journey: Prototype

While testing a prototype based on one feature, the user journey allows us to create an account of the steps and course of actions. This helps to clarify what needs to be done to simplify the user journey and test the flow of the screens on the prototypes.

EXAMPLE 2: CALENDAR BOOKING

The booking system in Figure 8-3 is far too complex and needs to be simplified. We can also identify several blockers. This was an early prototype, and it is quite common to have many issues at first. The purpose of testing the user journey is to draw an account of what works and what doesn't work.

Calendar booking

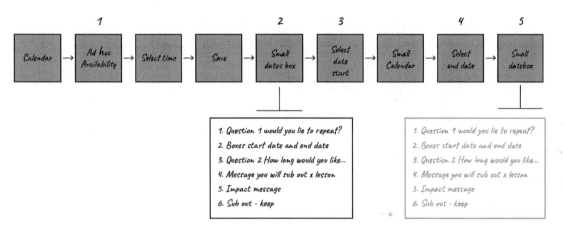

Figure 8-3. *User journey calendar booking*

User Journey: Build Product

You can test the user journey when the product is built or when it's live. It is essential to test it to find out whether there are any blockers. I recommend testing the user journey for the following reasons:

- To evaluate the current service from end to end

- To evaluate the service before release/live

EXAMPLE 3: REGISTRATION E-COMMERCE

This e-commerce user journey has three blockers that will prevent the user from registering (Figure 8-4). In the presentation of the results, the screen with the details of the issues needs to be described.

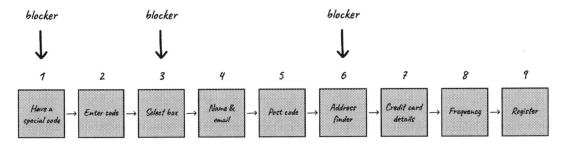

Figure 8-4. *User journey that shows blockers*

Persona

There is a difference between a user profile and a user persona. A user profile is a set characteristics based on demographics, job role, age, the industry the user is working in, how much money they are spending on specific products, what their socio-economics background is, which devices they use, etc.

A persona is a typical user who has specific characteristics such are interests, goals, behavior, attitude, habits, etc., that could be identified across several users. A persona is *not* a real user, it is *not* a case study, and it is *not* an imaginative character. A persona is based on systematic behaviors, motivation, and user needs that we have identified in our data. Personas help to understand user needs and behaviors toward a product.

For example, after conducting some interviews followed by some user testing sessions with the internal staff of a company in which we were creating a new internal communication, we identified five systematic behaviors (see Figure 8-5).

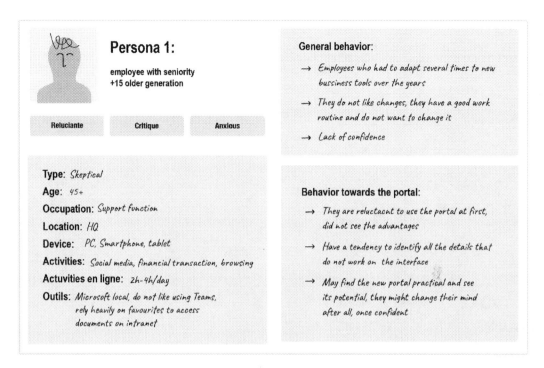

Figure 8-5. *Persona*

Deliverables and Presenting the Findings

I recommend documenting the findings in a presentation, following this format:

1. **Title:** The title slide should state the name of the project and have the date and the name of the researcher (Figure 8-6).

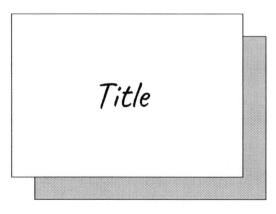

Figure 8-6. *Title slide for presentation*

2. **Table of contents:** This is useful to give some indication to the audience about what the presentation will cover. Also, it will help people to scan quickly the presentation if they are looking for a specific section (Figure 8-7).

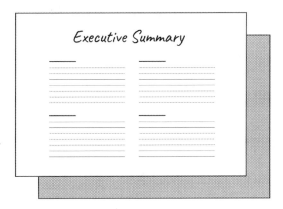

Figure 8-7. *Table of contents presentation*

3. **Executive summary:** This should restate the project aims, the participants, and the main findings (Figure 8-8).

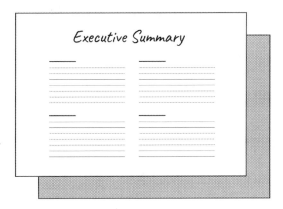

Figure 8-8. *Executive summary presentation*

4. **Background:** This slide provides some background information about the project, the product, etc. (Figure 8-9). It is useful if people are not familiar with the project. It is important to add a few pieces of information related to the product, such as why they decided to create the product, etc.

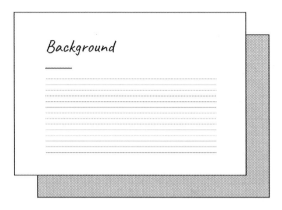

Figure 8-9. *Background slide*

5. **Aims/objectives of the project:** This slide must state the aims and the objectives of the project. This will frame the scope of the project (Figure 8-10).

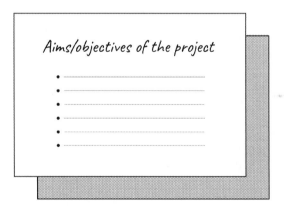

Figure 8-10. *Aims and objectives slides*

6. **Approach:** Stating the approach is important. This will help the audience to understand how user research works as well as provide the information if another researcher wants to do further research or review what has been done (Figure 8-11).

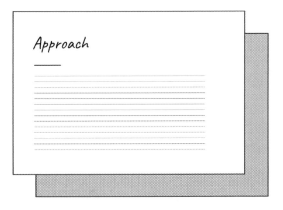

Figure 8-11. *Approach slide*

7. **Participants:** This slide gives some information about the
    participants who took part in the research, how many, some of
    their demographics or specificities, location, age, device usage,
    etc. (Figure 8-12).

Figure 8-12. *Participants slide*

8. **Research methods:** It is important for the audience to understand
    the research methods that were used to conduct the research, and
    it shows some structure and professionalism (Figure 8-13).

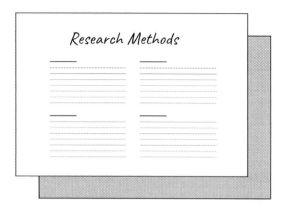

Figure 8-13. *Research method slide*

9. **Persona:** Presenting personas or restating personas that were already developed really helps the audience to understand the user's motivation and behavior (Figure 8-14).

Figure 8-14. *Persona slide*

10. **User journey or processes:** Drawing an account of the user journey that has been tested or identified through the research is essential to help the team and the audience to visualize the process to use the product and service (Figure 8-15).

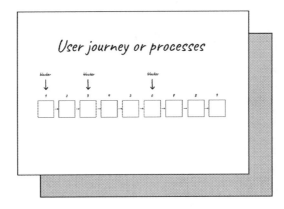

Figure 8-15. *User journey slide*

11. **Screens tested one-by-one, with feedback and recommendations:** Presenting every screen on a slide allows you to describe how the user interacted with the product and also highlight when something is not working (Figure 8-16 and Figure 8-17). This, supported with some quotes, really helps the audience understand what is happening, especially if there is a blocker. This slide helps the team to go back and work on a solution.

Figure 8-16. *Screen analysis*

2.18 Book a flight Paris Barcelona - Payment price details

✳ Participants were not happy about the extra charges especially the card one

✳ They find that the difference between the first price proposed and the one at the end of the process has increased dramatically and this will probably stop them to complete booking

✳ Only one participant knew that the platform did not charge the "frais de gestion" when flight booked between 3-6 am

 " It starts at $272 and ends at $324 with management fees of $52. The price is excessive and I'm going back"

 " It really annoys me, (that piss me off) it should be indicated earlier and now I'm going on another site to compare prices and charges"

Figure 8-17. *Details of one-by-one screen*

12. **Unexpected findings:** At some point in the project, the research may identify something that was unexpected, such as the need for an integration that was forgotten or a user need that will have a massive impact. This slide is to make the findings more visible (Figure 8-18).

Unexpected findings

- _____
- _____
- _____
- _____
- _____

Figure 8-18. *Unexpected finding slide*

13. **Quantitative data (if available):** The audience always likes to see some graphs. This is why I recommend presenting some graphs with the quantitative data that you have gathered (Figure 8-19).

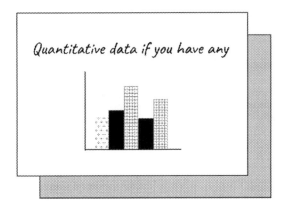

Figure 8-19. *Quantitative data findings*

14. **SUS if it was a user testing:** The SUS results are always good at tracking information, especially if you want to show some progress or issues in your product (Figure 8-20).

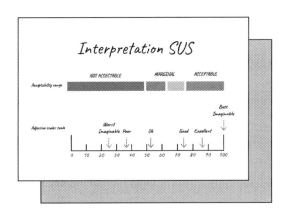

Figure 8-20. *SUS interpretation slide*

15. **Summary of the findings:** Reiterating the findings is always appreciated by the stakeholders/audience because with user research generally we have a lot of insight to share. The summary slide is a nice reminder (Figure 8-21).

Summary of the findings

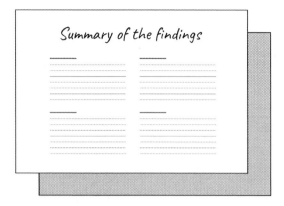

Figure 8-21. *Summary of the findings*

16. **List of the recommendations:** The recommendations (Figure 8-22) can be organized by priority using a severity scale.

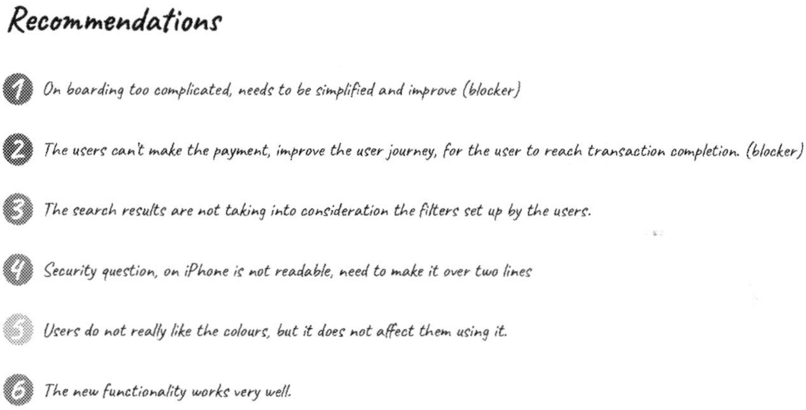

Recommendations
1 On boarding too complicated, needs to be simplified and improve (blocker)
2 The users can't make the payment, improve the user journey, for the user to reach transaction completion. (blocker)
3 The search results are not taking into consideration the filters set up by the users.
4 Security question, on iPhone is not readable, need to make it over two lines
5 Users do not really like the colours, but it does not affect them using it.
6 The new functionality works very well.

Figure 8-22. *Recommendations*

17. **Conclusion:** A conclusion helps to present what you plan to do next (Figure 8-23).

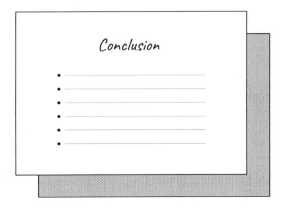

Figure 8-23. *Conclusion slide*

Summary

This chapter explained the method that we use to analyze qualitative data from contextual inquiries, interviews, and user testing. We also reviewed the following:

- The different steps to go through during the analysis

- The importance of going back to the raw data

- The main deliverables (user journey, persona, screen-by-screen analysis, etc.)

- The format and the different slides to present user research findings

CHAPTER 9

Participant Recruitment, Ethics, and Accessibility

This chapter talks about the participants who are taking part in user research. How do we recruit them, and which code of conduct do we have to respect? Knowing that the field of UX/user research is still in its early stages, we don't have a user research society yet that provides guidance to follow.

Doing user research involves real users. On many occasions, stakeholders or companies think that they are the users, or sometimes they say that they know their users. Stakeholders' motivations are often based on marketing or business perspective.

If we want to produce a successful product, we need to make sure the product is easy to use, as well as meets customer expectations. Meeting business needs and goals is important. Nevertheless, it is crucial to find the right balance between user needs and business needs. We may not be able to please every user, but we at least need to make sure that we are meeting the user needs of the majority of our population or audience/users.

The role of a user researcher would not exist without the users. To conduct any user research, we need users, namely, participants to take part in our study. Both the quantitative research and qualitative research methods require participants. This is what we'll look at in this chapter:

- Identify the participants.

- Emphasize the importance of including people with special needs and accessibility requirements.

- Review the ethics and what they involve.

© Emmanuelle Savarit 2020
E. Savarit, *Practical User Research*, https://doi.org/10.1007/978-1-4842-5596-4_9

Who Are the Users?

Before starting any research, it is essential to understand who your users are.

Using real users for user research is fundamental. I cannot even count the number of times I have arrived in a new organization and realized that it tests all its products with internal staff. I cannot say it enough: staff, stakeholders, and family members are not the right participants to take part in user research, unless the product is for internal staff such as an intranet. Employees are the wrong participants; they are completely biased.

Identifying Which Participant Profiles You Want

In user research, we are not interested in the demographics, job role, etc. We are interested in participants' motivation, in other words, their behavior while using your product. We recommend that you take the time to identify who the different categories of users are and see how they interact with your product or service. It is not always easy to identify the right users who should be testing your product when you have many clients.

Identifying How Many Participants You Need

The sample size in user research is an important debate; I have been fighting for many years to make sure that organizations are using enough participants for their research. Often, when I start a new project, I look at previous research and see that decisions were made based on research involving only five participants. This is probably because the Nielson Norman Group has said throughout their training and communication that five participants are good enough.

Quantitative Research

It is imperative to decide on the sample size, whether it is quantitative or qualitative research. It always depends on what you are testing and at which stage you are in your product development.

For quantitative data, I recommend more than 1,000 respondents for a survey. For the analytics, I expect a lot of traffic to see what is going on.

Qualitative Research

For qualitative research, it is a bit tricky. I am in total opposition to the five participants recommendation from Nielson Normal Group. To have reliable results with qualitative research, I recommend a minimum of eight people if you are conducting user testing every sprint (every two weeks for a period of eight to twelve weeks) and you are in the alpha or beta phase).

When your product is live or in private beta and if you want to test the end-to-end journey before release, I recommend between 12 to 24 participants. You are not going to test the product with only one category of users. You should also consider their location and the profile, meaning if they are customers or not, if they are computer savvy, how often they use your product, etc. Also, if you want to create some persona, you need more than five participants. The fact is that we are looking for a systematic pattern across the participants, so if while analyzing the data you don't have enough participants, you will not identify the pattern.

Recruiting Participants

Before starting to recruit your participants, you should start by creating a screener. A *screener* is a series of questions that help you to identify the right participants for your research. The screener has a series of questions related to demographics, technology usage, and the product. For example, if you want to test an app for kids, make sure the participants have children. Or if the app that you are testing is for Android, make sure you have Android users. It may look simple and like common sense, but I remember testing an app for iPhone in Hong Kong several years ago. When I took the subway, I realized that I couldn't see any iPhones. It seems that the stakeholder made the wrong call when they decided to build a product for the iPhone.

If you need to recruit some participants for your research, first you need to know if you have some budget or resources internally to help you. Recruiting participants is time-consuming, and it is not easy. If you have the budget and if the type of participants you need is straightforward, I recommend you use a participant recruitment agency.

For quantitative research, we need participants to respond to our survey. Having access to a panel is useful, but you have to keep in mind that the panel may spend a lot of time answering the questions. You may be able to build an internal panel; often they are your clients, but you may miss out on the nonclient users. You can find some specialized panel to answer your survey. It is worth the investment, since the goal of a survey in user research and UX is to validate some assumptions, but most of the time it is to validate qualitative findings. Getting a larger sample should make the results more reliable.

For qualitative research, finding the relevant participants is fundamental because we are using a smaller sample; having the wrong participants is a waste of time and money, and this will affect the results dramatically. Here are some examples:

- You are launching a new app for frequent flyers and one of your participants rarely flies.

- You test a product to learn a foreign language and you realize that the participant is bilingual.

- You are testing a service for car owners and the participant does not even have his driving license.

Having the right participants is essential.

Screener

Before starting to recruit participants for qualitative research, you need to prepare a screener, as shown in Figure 9-1. A screener is a quick survey/questionnaire that helps to identify the relevant participants based on specific criteria (see the screener example in Appendix A).

If you don't have the internal capability to prepare a screener, you can ask the recruitment agency to prepare it for you. In terms of the screener, it is essential to stick with the participants that you want at first; then if the agency has difficulties recruiting them, you can widen the criteria.

Once you have your screener, you can start recruiting your participants. You need to have a clear schedule, slots for the sessions, or days for the fieldwork.

To recruit participants, there are several possibilities; it depends on your budget, the resources available to recruit, and the specificity of your participant requirements.

Screener

Introduction

Good morning, my name is _____.

I work n the behalf of [Name of the company] we are looking for participant to take part of our research.

[brief details about the project]

Does this sound like something that interests you?

If yes

Do you have a few moments for me to ask you a few questions?

General Questions

What is your gender?   Male   Female   Other

Have you participated in a [focus group, user research, usability testing, customer interviews test] in the past six months?

yes   no

Do you, or does anyone in your home, work [in market research, user research or UX? or the sector of activity of the project?]

yes   no

What is your age group?

18 to 25
26 to 39
40 to 59
60 - to 74;
75 and older

What is your household income?

under 25 000
between 25 000 to 35 000
Between 35

Which of the following best describes your race or ethnic group? [e.g., Caucasian, Asian, Black/African-American, Latino/a or Hispanic, etc.]

Professional Demographics
[Customize this to reflect your site's primary audience]

What is your current position and title?

How long have you been working in this current position?

Where do you currently work?

Which of the following describes your highest level of education?

Some high school
high school graduate/GED
some college
Graduate BA/BSc
Postgraduate (MSc/MA/PhD)
Other (explain)

Computer Expertise ?

Which devices to you own?

computer?
tablet
smartphone?
are you Mac or PC?

[If none of them, terminate unless you want to test with someone without any previous experience.]

Figure 9-1. Screener

Using a Participant Recruitment Agency

There are several participant recruitment agencies; some used to recruit for market research, while others specialize in user/UX research. In the United Kingdom, you can use People, Saros, or TestingTime. Some labs also offer the service to recruit participants for a fee. Agencies charge between £40 to £150 ($50-$185) per participant depending on the specific requirements needed.

I recommend shopping around to find out which agency will be the best for your project. Some agencies are not specialized enough to find specific participants, such as professionals or people with special needs.

Once you find an agency, you need to make sure they understand what you are looking for, so give them your screeners. Also, check with them to see what happens if a participant cancels or is delayed for the session. How do they handle the situation?

Internal Client List

If your customers are specialized professionals, you may be better off asking your marketing department, if you have one, to send an email to their client list. The purpose of the email is to ask your clients if they will be interested in taking part in the research. If they show you some interest, you or the marketing team can contact them and go through the screener. Don't forget that the internal client list will only provide current clients, so try to see how you can get a wider audience.

Advertising

Sometimes, to get specific participants, recruitment agencies do not always meet your needs. They may not have in their database the specific users you are looking for. Therefore, another alternative is to put an ad in a local paper or on social media or go through an association. If you are managing your recruitment internally, you need to make sure you have dedicated resources that can help as the researcher will not have the time to handle everything. Managing recruitment is time-consuming and involves a lot of administration/emails. You can use a research assistant to help you with recruitment.

NICHE PARTICIPANT

To recruit businesses when I was working for the Skills Funding Agency, I used a chamber of commerce. I looked at the member's list, shortlisted the ones I was interested in, and sent out emails one by one (not a batch email). I also went to Business Network International (BNI) morning meet-ups to find possible participants. Finding the right participants is hard and time-consuming.

Professional Participants

You need to be vigilant. Certain people are "professionals." They want to participate because many researchers offer a financial incentive. Avoid these people as much as possible (sometimes they even use a different identity).

Incentives

A voluntary participant is rare to find unless the product that you are trying to build is going to change their life. You can still find participants such as teachers, nurses, passionate people, or people who are highly involved in the community and will do the testing without any incentive.

I recommend giving at least a voucher to every participant. Cash incentives are also used. You need to think carefully about how much you are going to give. Just as an idea, some agencies provide from £30 to £150 ($35-$185) in cash, bank transfer, or vouchers. Sometimes we also offer to participants to give their incentive to the charity of their choice. Make sure the participants sign the document stating that they received a cash or voucher incentive. Your company's financial department or your accountant will ask for it.

Taxation on Incentive

Taxation depends on the country where the participant resides; it is always important to check how it will affect the participant's income tax or benefits.

No-Shows

It is always possible that a participant, even if the agency confirmed the attendance, decides at the last minute to not show up.

What can you do to prevent a no-show? Always stays in touch with the participants. If you are using a recruitment agency, check with them first about which communications they have sent to the participants such as a booking letter/email, consent form, and instructions to get to the lab if it is the case. It is the responsibility of the recruitment agency to provide you with the relevant participants and to make sure they will show up for the session.

When you are doing the recruitment internally, I recommend calling the participant the day before and sending a message with all the directions and information at least two hours before the session. Each time you contact them, remind them that if they want to cancel, they should inform you ASAP to allow time to find a substitute participant. Try to have backup participants just in case; you always have the possibility of a no-show.

Accessibility and Vulnerable Participants

Accessibility and assisted digital technologies are a fundamental matter. Many organizations do not realize that it is essential to make their website, platform, or software accessible to all.

Gov.uk has been an innovator in that sense as it systematically requires participants with individual needs to test their products/services.

There has been an increase in interest recently concerning accessibility, probably because of the recent Domino Pizza lawsuit. Customers with visual impairment sued Domino Pizza because its website was not accessible and excluded them from placing an order. Not only did Domino Pizza have to fix its website to make it accessible, but it had to pay legal compensation to the customers who sued.

Many people think accessibility is only for a minority group, but 20 percent of the population needs some accessibility accommodations. Making a website or a digital product accessible means that people with a disability can use it in terms of perception, comprehension, navigation, and interaction.

Organizations need to start thinking about accessibility not only as something good for their reputation, but as good for their ROI since more people will use their product if it is accessible. For example, Barclays made 80 percent of its cash machines accessible. More and more organizations have some accessibility teams now.

- Don't wait until the end of the project. If you are working on accessibility from the start, it will cost you $30,000. If you wait until the end, it will cost you $300,000.

- Make accessibility everyone's responsibility.

- Don't wait until you get bad press.

- Include accessibility into your guidelines and your branding.

- Test your product with real users who have accessibility needs (people who use assistive technology, screen magnifiers, etc.).

Assisted Digital

Assisted digital is the alternative route that enable users which are not computer savvy to use your product and service. It could be to offer self-serve devices, such as an iPad or a computer station for people who do not have digital tools. It could also be supported by providing advice on how to use the digital service. Some people are capable, but do not feel confident enough to use a digital service.

The British government has worked hard to make the assisted digital route a must for any citizen-facing product (Figure 9-2). I highly recommend taking a look at Gov.uk's blog on assisted digital and its guidelines.

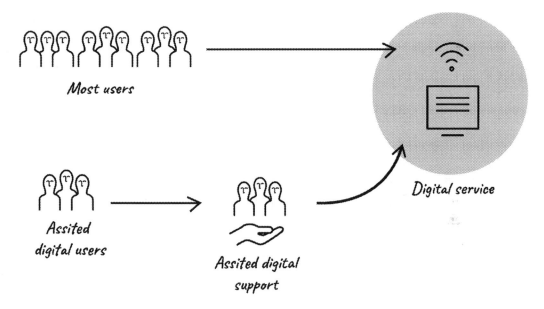

Figure 9-2. Assisted digital www.Gov.uk

It's important to understand your users and their needs, so let's explore some key facts in the following sections.

Elderly People

Ten million people in the United Kingdom are older than 65 years old, which is one in six of the UK population, and by 2025 it will be one in four. They may have issues adopting and adapting to new technology such as computers, apps, and wearable devices as their ability, hearing, and sight deteriorate.

These are some of their challenges:

- Not computer savvy

- Difficulties or inability to use hands, which could affect the usage of a mouse or keyboard

- Limited comprehension, memory loss, and attention deficit

- Low attention span for cognitive overload (too much information)

- Hearing difficulties

Disabled People

Since Britain came out victorious of the 2016 Paralympic Games, accessibility to sports in the United Kingdom is well known. Why not think of digital inclusion as part of your business culture? Companies such as the BBC, as well as Governmental Digital Strategy, emphasize the accessibility of their websites; 83 percent of the disabled community became disabled later in life, following an illness or an accident.

Visual Impairment

About 1.87 million people have sight loss (low vision and color blindness) in the United Kingdom, which has a significant impact on their daily lives.

Here are some of their challenges:

- They use assistive technology, such as screen readers or screen magnifiers.

- They use a Braille device.

- They cannot perceive the differences between some colors.

- They need to make things bigger and cannot read text that has poor contrast.

About 10 million in the United Kingdom have some hearing loss, which is one in six of the population.

Hearing Impairment

People with Hearing impairment makes it difficult to access online lectures/training, to access 235 multimedia content, and to participate in a discussion. Here are some possible solutions:

- Voice recognition software
- Sign language
- Audio accessibility

Disabled People

About 57 percent of disabled people in the United Kingdom have mobility issues, which has an impact on their abilities to move, coordinate, and control their movement when performing tasks on digital products or services.

Some of their challenges include the following:

- Difficulties or inability to use their hands that will affect usage of a mouse or keyboard
- Slow movements that require more time to complete a task
- Required to use an alternative to hands (feet, arm, elbow, head)

Learning Difficulties

About 1.5 million people in the United Kingdom have learning difficulties. One in four will experience a mental health condition. Cognitive impairment includes memory, perception, problem-solving, conceptualization, and attention deficits (autism, brain injury, Parkinson's disease, Alzheimer's, dyslexia, mental retardation, etc.).

Here are some of their challenges:

- Low comprehension
- Difficulties understanding content
- Reading difficulties
- Short-term memory loss
- Limited attention span

Nondigital Users

In the United Kingdom, 12 million adults lack basic digital skills. This part of the population is not able to use digital services or products on their own.

Here are their challenges:

- Lack of digital skills

- Low confidence

- No Internet access

- No access to computer or devices

- Need support by phone, web chat, or in person

Recruiting Special Needs Participants

People with accessibility needs, or children, are vulnerable people. We need to be very careful (see the "Ethics" section) to recruit participant with special needs. It is not always the easiest. We have to be creative as some participant recruitment agencies are not doing their job to recruit these participants.

Recruiting participants with special needs is challenging, but some participant recruitment agencies specialize in this category of participants. Still, they quickly give up, as it is time-consuming, and participants need a lot of support and reassurance throughout the recruitment process.

It is possible to go through community websites, meet-ups, or social media. These sometimes are an excellent way to find the right people.

You can also use a specialized agency to do an audit of your site or use automatic accessibility software to test it. I find that doing testing with people with special needs always bring better insights and that we manage to capture even more issues. It is also instructive to watch people with special needs interacting with your product. Keep in mind that people with special needs are vulnerable, and you need to respect their vulnerability and make sure you use ethics and respect a code of conduct.

Ethics

Before doing any research with a human participant no-show, we have to respect ethical and legal concerns as well as follow a code of conduct. It is our responsibility as researchers to protect our participants and their data.

You can't collect data without participant consent. You have to make sure that the participant gives their permission before starting the research.

You have to provide enough information to the participants, especially when you are planning to use a qualitative research methodology, for them to understand that the research is anonymous and that they have the right to withdraw at any time. You also need to make sure that the participant isn't distressed during the session. Sometimes, we may ask a question that could affect the participant. The participant must understand that they don't have to reply to the question if they are not comfortable. Additionally, their participation in the research is voluntary, and we can't force them to respond to our questions.

VULNERABLE PEOPLE

I have seen researchers (actually they were not researchers with proper experience) who were doing a home visit to test a service. The participants were older adults, and one of the participants got tired. The session was supposed to be an hour and a half, but the participant was too tired to continue after 45 minutes.

There were two visitors in the participant's home, and one of them wanted to continue, since they needed the data. The other one who had a psychology background told the first researcher that they had to respect the code of conduct and ethics.

Using the Data

During contextual inquiries or user testing sessions, we tend to take pictures and also video record the interaction. To record the data, we need to ask the participant to give consent. If the participant doesn't want to be recorded, you can't record the session. They also have the right to say at the end of the session if they do not want us to use the data.

I find that giving some clarification to the participant is important, such as mentioning that the data is just for research purposes and it will not be shared. It is just for analysis purposes. In this case, a participant usually doesn't have any issue giving consent. Not only that, but the participant also has to give consent to take part in the research. We also need to know to which extent we can use the data. Especially when we use audio, still images, and video recordings, we need to ask them if they are happy for us to use the recordings in front of our team (product team), to share them with stakeholders, or to use them at a conference. Before using any data at a conference, we have to make sure we've gotten the full consent for that.

As a researcher, we need to make sure that we respect the participant and their privacy and confidentiality, communities, and values. As a researcher, we have to show empathy, sympathy, generosity, openness, distress tolerance, commitment, and courage. We need to make sure we do not cause any harm to a participant.

You have to follow a code of conduct; I am following the British Psychological Society's Code of Conduct, which includes the Code of Human Research Ethics and Practice Guidelines.

The highlights of the Code of Conduct are

- Respect

- Competence

- Responsibility

- Integrity

Confidentiality

"Subject to the requirements of legislation, including the Data Protection Act, information obtained from and about a participant during an investigation is confidential unless otherwise agreed in advance. Investigators who are put under pressure to disclose confidential information should draw this point to the attention of those exerting such pressured." (BPS Code of Conduct)

Vulnerable Participants

Some participants, such as children, are not able to give consent; the consent needs to be given by their legal representative.

Participants with Limited Capabilities

Some adult participants may not be able to give consent themselves, or they may not understand what the session will be about. Their legal proxy should provide the consent.

If someone can't sign the consent form, I recommend recording the consent. Or if the participant is doing a remote session, you should be sending the consent form before the sessions and make sure you get it signed before you start the session.

The Right to Withdraw at Any Time

I often go back to the consent at the beginning of the session and emphasize the fact that if the participant feels stressed or uncomfortable at any time, I will stop. We also use a nondisclosure agreement (NDA), which is a form that participants have to sign before taking part in the research. This is to protect the company, especially when we test some new concept and prototypes. We do not want anyone to know about what we are testing, especially not the competitors.

Summary

This chapter explained the importance of recruiting the right participants. After all, they are at the heart of our research. The following are some basic process to follow:

- Identify the right participants for the research and how to recruit them.

- Include participants with accessibility requirements or that require assistance while using your product.

- Take an ethical approach and respect participants by following a code a conduct (consent form, right to withdraw, etc.).

CHAPTER 10

Using Your New Skills in the Real World

This chapter will present different project briefs. You can use them to put into practice what you have learned in this book. The briefs come from real projects that I worked on over the last few years. I will try to give you the context while obviously keeping the name of the companies anonymous. I can't give you the official results, which were in the report, as I need to respect client confidentiality. Still, I try to give you enough information in terms of the approach, the methods, and the participants. I also give a high-level overview of the outcome where you will find an overview of the methods, the processes that I used, and the main deliverable. The point is for you to see the systematic approach I have used in real-world user research.

The ten briefs are covering the following:

Brief 1: E-commerce subscription service

Brief 2: New intranet and communication tools for internal users

Brief 3: Integration of a new acquisition onto a financial platform

Brief 4: New banking apps in Asia

Brief 5: New website for a small business

Brief 6: Travel apps for iPad in France

Brief 7: Ops portal

Brief 8: Hardware and software for children

Brief 9: Survey with teachers

Brief 10: Redesign of the My Account section of a gambling website

© Emmanuelle Savarit 2020
E. Savarit, *Practical User Research*, https://doi.org/10.1007/978-1-4842-5596-4_10

Brief 1: E-commerce Subscription Service

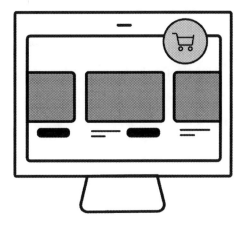

A company that is several years old offers snacks delivered via mail. It is a subscription service. Customers receive their box once a week, without knowing in advance which snacks they will get. Users can subscribe to the product by going on the company's website through their computer, tablet, or smartphone.

The style of the website is trendy, with great colors and images. The client spent a lot of money on a designer who helped them with the branding, the website, etc.

The look and feel of their website is great, with beautiful images and a great design. The people in charge of the site are in the marketing department, which has five to six people.

When they came to us, they had launched some new features and realized they were not doing very well (e.g., one-off delivery to a friend; breakfast cereal box subscription).

They were under pressure from their investors. They needed to understand why their new products were not performing as well as the initial product. They also wanted to find out what to do to improve the performance.

After running a kickoff meeting with the stakeholders, we got the following information:

- They wanted to test the user journey of how to send a box to a friend (audience = current client).

- They wanted to identify how the product was perceived.

- They wanted to evaluate the current user journey to subscribe, as well as the journey to order new products.

- They wanted to find out why people were not buying their products (nonclient audience).

- We would have access to the client list.

- We had four weeks to complete the research project.

- They had a budget to give participants incentives and to use a recruitment agency for the nonclient participants.

- We had access to the analytics.

- We could use rooms in their office to run the sessions.

Here are some questions to help you plan your research (these could be used for every brief):

- What is the aim of the project?

- What does the business want to do?

- Which phase are you in (discovery, alpha, beta, live)?

- What are the research questions?

- How long do you have to complete your project?

- Which research method will you use?

- Who are the users?

- How many users will you need for the projects?

- How are you going to recruit the participants?

- What is your budget?

- Did you prepare your research plan with a gantt chart?

- Do you have all your material ready?

Aims/Objectives

The project was in the live phase. The objectives were as follows:

- To get feedback from the interviews and from testing to provide a practical insight to shape the direction when improving the website

- To identify whether there are some usability issues that need to be fixed or improved

- To assess how users may perceive the website

- To assess if there are different needs for existing customers versus first-time visitors

Approach

Face-to face user testing sessions were undertaken at the client office. We used two rooms, one for the sessions and the other one for the clients to watch the session, as we were projecting the screen and the video though Apple TV.

The format of the sessions was based on a script (discussion guide) prepared by the researcher.

The format of the interview was informal and semistructured. The interview directive was just to keep the interview on track.

Sessions lasted one hour based on the following:

- A semistructured interview (demographic and behavioral)

- 17 tasks to be completed by the participants

- SUS questionnaires that were sent to participants to be filled out online after the session

Participants

Ten participants were recruited through a recruitment agency; a screener was prepared to select the correct users.

We also provided a contact list of current subscribers who would be interested in taking part in the research.

- Five subscribers (three female and two male)

- Five nonsubscribers (three female and two male)

We gave them a £50 ($60 USD) incentive to thank them for their time and participation.

All participants were iPhone users.

Methodologies

All sessions were video recorded with Silverback software. The screen of the laptop was displayed on the researcher's MacBook Air by using AirPlay, which enabled the researcher to record the MacBook Air's screen with Silverback.

Notes were taken during the session.

The notes were summarized in an Excel spreadsheet, and after the user testing, the video files were reviewed and added to the spreadsheet.

Thematic analysis was used to analyze the outcome of the session, with data being coded and organized into categories. Similarities in themes were identified across participants and across sections of the product tested (e.g. website).

Overview of the Findings

The findings included the following:

- Issues based on feedback and task evaluation were reported using a problem severity rating of Severe, High, Medium, or Good (Figure 10-1).

- Three Severe issues were reported: asking the noncustomers for payment details too early in the process, asking again for the payment details of the current subscribers to order nonregular boxes such as gifts, and there were some issues in the user journey.

- Five High issues were reported, generally related to buttons, user journey, clarity in communication of the concept, and terminology used.

- 13 Medium noncritical issues were also reported.

- The system usability score of the website was excellent.

- The visual design, layout, colors, and icons received good feedback. We also identified some user needs that could open new business opportunities.

- Recommendations and quotes from participants were also reported.

Severity scale

○ *Severe:* An emergency condition that caused the website to fail or caused customer data to be lost or destroyed. A showstopper usability bug can also be one that is likely to cause frequent data integrity errors. There is no workaround to there problems. A key feature needed by many customers is not in the system. The problem causes users irritation and will make them leave the platform.

○ *High:* A serious condition that impairs the operation, or continued operations, of one or more product fuctions and cannot be easily circumvented or avoided. The sofware does nor prevent the user from making serious mistakes. The usability problem is frequent is frequent, persistent and affects many users. There is a serious violations of standars. The problem causes users confusion or irritation.

○ *Medium:* A non critical, limited problem (no data lost or system failure), it does not hinder operation and can be temporarily circumvented or avoided. The problem causes users moderate confusion or irritation. Minor inconsistencies result in small authentic issues.

○ *Good:* No problem, positive outcome

Figure 10-1. *Severity scale*

Brief 2: Eye-Tracking User Testing Session

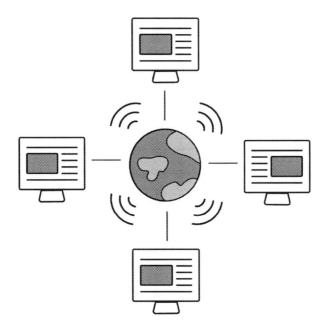

A global company, which is part of a Fortune Global 500 company, was currently going through a digital transformation. The internal communication team had a great ambition to improve things. The IT team was migrating to Office 365 as well as reorganizing their data on SharePoint. They had a tech company specializing in SharePoint that had been commissioned to support them. The communication team wanted to create a new interactive intranet, with some communities to facilitate communication across employees as well as facilitating daily work.

A discovery was made with an external agency that highlighted high-level business needs. During the alpha phase, we reran some workshops to clarify the business needs and to work on some wireframes and the design to customize the SharePoint intranet. This involved many features such as customized news depending on the business unit, as well as access to documents, tools, community chat and groups, etc. The tech company built the front end and put it in front of users (staff). The alpha had the integration of these three features:

- The home page

- The news page with three different types of news

- The community/group that enabled the employee to create, chat, and communicate as well as socialize through the intranet

At the end of the alpha, we realized that employees liked the concept. Still, the customization was going to be a burden financially with a maintenance cost every time Microsoft did a software update. We reviewed and evaluated other possibilities. The client went for a customized layer on SharePoint. The supplier (layer) created an MVP and completed the migration of the content.

We got the following information after the kickoff meeting:

- 200 staff members took part in the private beta.

- 28 participants took part in the user testing session (some were in the main office, and some were in remote offices).

- We wanted to test the overall concept.

- We wanted to test different user journeys such as search, customizing news, and tools etc.

- We wanted to test the layout, the design, etc.

- We wanted to test the usability.

Aims/Objectives

The project was in the beta phase. These were the objectives:

- Understanding who the users are

- Understanding how they are using the new intranet

- Understanding which information they are looking for on the intranet

- Understanding their frustrations around the service

- Getting feedback from employees about the new intranet interface (from 28 participants as well as the other 200 who took part in the private beta)

- Identifying whether there were some usability issues that needed to be fixed or improved

- Getting insight around navigation, design, search, the relevance of the content, etc.

- Assessing the user journeys

Approach

We organized user testing sessions that included face-to-face user testing with eye-tracking, as well as remote user testing sessions for the participants who were in other offices.

A discussion guide was created by the researcher that included several tasks such as customization of their landing page with their most commonly used tools. Participants also had to create a community, take a picture with their phone, and post a note on the group through the mobile app.

A SUS questionnaire was also done with the 28 user testing participants and even with the other participants of the pilot.

A satisfaction questionnaire was also used with the other 172 participants, to get a wider sample.

Participants

The participants included the following:

- 28 participants across six different business units in different locations

- 170 participants across the same six business units

Methodologies

The following were the methodologies.

User Testing

Face-to-face and remote user testing sessions were conducted. We used Tobii eye-tracking software (`https://www.tobiipro.com/sprint/`) for the face-to-face sessions and Zoom for the remote sessions.

The format of the interview was informal and semistructured. The interview directive was just to keep the interview on track.

The notes were summarized in an Excel spreadsheet. The video files were reviewed, and comments were added to the spreadsheet. Thematic analysis was used to examine the outcome of the sessions. Data was coded and organized into categories. Similarities in themes could be identified across participants, sections of the task, and user testing sessions.

Survey

A questionnaire of 20 satisfaction questions was prepared to get feedback from the 200 employees who took part in the private beta. We also asked all the participants to complete the SUS questionnaires, which were sent to them to be filled in online after the session. Figure 10-2 shows the interpretation results.

Overview of the Findings

The findings included the following:

- Five personas, reflecting motivation and user behavior

- User journey to show how a user performs the tasks

- Results based on all the sections of the intranet

- The SUS scores

- Survey results

- Recommendations on how to improve the intranet, also by using color coding from the severity scale

Interpretation SUS

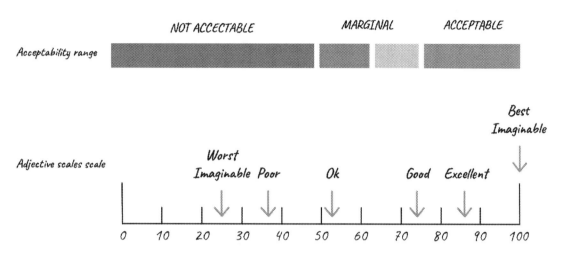

Figure 10-2. *System Usability Scale interpretation table*

Brief 3: A Large Financial Organization Wants to Integrate a New Product into Its Current Financial Platform

The client was a multinational company that just bought several companies that offer data on commodities for financial services. The client wanted to integrate the data into its current financial platform. Before doing so, they needed to understand the users, their needs, what the products were, and how they are going to integrate them with the current product. Since so many questions needed answers, a discovery was required to come up with an integration strategy.

We got the following information after the kickoff meeting:

- The client bought four different companies.

- The end users are analysts and traders across the world.

- We do not have a clear account of the data and the products.

- We need to understand the users, how they use the current products, and how the integration will affect them.

- We need to understand what the format of the data is (digital, book, report, or something else)?

- The sales and marketing departments could help to recruit participants.

- They have a budget to pay incentives.

- Travel to some location was included in the budget.

- We needed to have a strategy at the end of the research for the integration.

Aims/Objectives

The project was in the discovery phase. These were the objectives:

- To have a clear idea of what the products are

- To understand who the users are and how they currently use the product

- To understand what the best solution would be to integrate the new product into the current financial platform

Approach

We conducted some fieldwork in the users' natural environment (contextual inquiry) to understand how users interact with the product during their daily work. Contextual inquiry/ethnography enabled us not only to capture how they were using the current product but also to identify the other tools/products they were using.

We organized 16 visits in different financial organizations in London and New York, as well as video conferences or phone interviews in Australia, South America, and Europe.

Participants

We identified users who were already subscribers of the financial platform and others who were just using the product A, B, C, or D. Users included the following:

- Portfolio managers, traders, analysts

We also wanted to understand the products and spoke with the following:

- Employees of the four companies that had been bought

- Salespeople from clients to understand their vision

Methodologies

Note and pictures were taken through the contextual inquiry, while interviews were recorded and transcribed using a transcription agency.

The notes were summarized in an Excel spreadsheet. The video files were reviewed, and comments were added to the spreadsheet. Thematic analysis was used to examine the outcome of the sessions. Data was coded and organized into categories. Similarities in themes were identified across participants.

Overview of the Findings

The findings included the following:

- We had a clear account of the users and created personas.

- We created a list of user needs.

- We understood the format and how they used the products.

- We had some ideas about the integration of some of the product.

- We identified some gaps in the market that our client could use to improve the offerings.

- We came up with issues related to the integration of some of the products.

- We had a list of other sources/tools/products that traders/analysts used to do their jobs.

Brief 4: iPhone Apps for Retail Banking in London and Asia

This client was one of the largest banks in the world. They had gone through a product redesign, and they commissioned a design agency to work on a prototype for their retail apps. They wanted to do some user testing.

We got the following information after the kickoff meeting:

- The top two locations of users are the United Kingdom and Asia.

- They tested the new desktop design in the United Kingdom.

- They didn't do a research discovery.

- The design agency did do some desk investigation.

- They had a budget to test in different locations.

- The marketing team could support user testing.

- They had a deadline for the launch of the apps.

- They did not have persona; they had marketing profiles.

Aims/Objectives

The project was in the alpha phase. A limitation was that no research had been done before. These were the objectives:

- To evaluate the prototype of the new retail apps in two locations, London and Hong Kong

- To understand if there were any cultural differences in terms of user needs

- To understand which functionalities users are looking for

- To understand which other apps are they using

- To evaluate usability issues, design, and navigation

Approach

Face-to face user testing sessions were undertaken, with 16 in London, for which we rented a room. We used Silverback to record the screen as well as the video of the participants.

Another 16 sessions were done in Hong Kong. We rented a lab with recording facilities and a viewing room. The moderator was Chinese, speaking Cantonese. A translator was also in the viewing room to translate the session simultaneously.

The format of the sessions was based on a script (discussion guide) prepared by the researcher and translated in Cantonese.

The format of the interview was informal and semistructured. The interview directive was just to keep the interview on track.

Sessions lasted one hour based on the following:

- A semistructured interview (demographic and behavioral)

- Several tasks that were asked of the participants

- SUS questionnaires that were sent to them to be filled in online after the session

Participants

The participants were as follows:

- We had 16 participants in London who had been customers for more than two years.

- We had 16 participants in Hong Kong who had been customers for more than two years.

- Some of the participants used other banks as well.

- We tried to get an equilibrium between male and female.

- All users were iPhone users.

Methodologies

Here are the methodologies used.

London

All sessions were video recorded with Silverback software and also with the lab recording facilities. The screen of the laptop was displayed on the researcher's MacBook Pro.

Asia

The screen of the iPhone was shared using Apple TV and projected on the wall, thus enabling the researchers, the translator, and the team to view at the same time what the user was doing. All sessions and the translation were also recorded.

Notes were taken during the sessions. The notes were summarized in an Excel spreadsheet, and after the user testing, video files were reviewed and added to the spreadsheet.

Thematic analysis was used to analyze the outcome of the session, with data being coded and organized into categories.

Similarities in themes could be identified across participants and across sections of the product tested (e.g. website).

Overview of the Findings

The findings included the following:

- We identified cross-cultural differences such as users from Hong Kong required other functionalities, since they have different user needs.

- We presented a list of user needs based on user personas and background.

- The user journey based on the tasks was successful.

- We identified issues related to functionality, design, and navigation.

- We listed features that users would like but were not present.

- Other bank app features.

- System Usability Scale score.

- Demographic information of participants.

- Recommendations associated with the problem severity rating.

Brief 5: A New Website for a Small Business

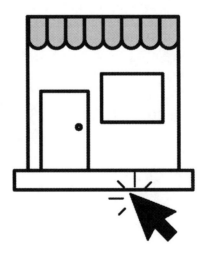

The client was a small business that was offering a service; it currently did not have a website and did not know where to start. The client wanted to commission a web design agency but needed some support before that.

We had a good relationship with the web agency, but they wanted the research to choose the structure, the layout, and the content that should be available on the site. It was a small business, and the budget is tight.

After the meeting with the owner of the business and with the web design agency, we knew the following:

- The web agency did not understand the business and what it was trying to sell.

- The owner of the business was very technical about her service and needed to simplify the content.

- The website purpose was a "vitrine" to provide information and to invite the client to contact the business to get their service.

- We had an idea of the branding and the colors that the client wanted to use.

- We also had someone working on the new logo.

Aims/Objectives

The project was in the discovery/alpha/beta/live phase. A limitation was that the budget was small. The objectives were as follows:

- To understand who the users are

- To understand what the client services are

- To provide insight to create wireframes

- To test the new website with real users

Approach

Because of the time constraints and the limited budget, we prepared a questionnaire for the business owner to fill in so we could understand the nature of the business, the offerings, and who the users were.

We organized a face-to-face meeting with the business owner to get more information about the business. Quick wireframes were done to look at the main structure of the site.

The web agency applied the recommendations. We did a review on a regular basis to make sure our recommendations were taken into consideration.

Once the website and the content were ready, we asked the business owner to help us get four or five clients to quickly test the online material.

We conducted some remote user testing (20 minutes maximum) just to get enough information to update the site.

We provided the main findings to the web design agency and helped them to improve the website until it was live.

Participants

The participants included the following:

- Business owner
- Clients

Methodologies

The methodologies included the following:

- Interview
- Questionnaire with open questions
- Site review
- Guerrilla remote testing (see Chapter 7)

Overview of the Findings

The findings included the following:

- We understood the business needs and the user needs.

- The content needed to be simplified.

- Images were carefully chosen to convey information.

- Visibility of the contacts information was presented in several location.

- The content and the explanation was simplified to provide more clarity.

- Users liked the new website.

Brief 6: Travel Apps for iPad in France

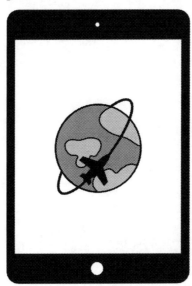

A client who owns an online travel agent product in France had launched an iPad app (MVP). The client did not do any formal user research; the only evaluation that was done was internal, and the client also monitored activities through the analytics. The analytics showed some poor performance and probably some usability issues.

The testing needed to be done by French users in France. They had some budget for recruitment and incentive, but not enough to rent a lab.

After the meeting with the product owner, we understood the following:

- They hadn't done any research before.

- The MVP was live.

- They had some analytics that showed that the app was not doing very well.

- They wanted to find out what was going on.

- They wanted to see how their product compared with the competitors.

Aims/Objectives

The project was in the live phase. These were the objectives:

- To gain feedback from the interviews and through user testing to provide practical insights to inform how to improve the MVP tablet web version

- To validate and identify design and usability issues that need improvement and may cause a lack of customer retention

- To assess how users may perceive and evaluate this new tablet version in comparison with the desktop version

- To evaluate how users may perceive this tablet web version in comparison with the competitor offerings

- To understand who the users are and how they behave toward an online travel agency

The overall project objective was to gather reliable data related to usability, user experience, and user perception of the "travel booking" MVP web tablet version and to provide recommendations.

Approach

Face-to face user testing sessions were undertaken in Paris at the client's office.

The format of the sessions was based on a script prepared by the researcher and translated into French.

The format of the interviews was informal and semistructured; the interview directive was just to keep the interview on track.

The sessions were based on the following:

- A semistructured interview (demographic and behavioral)

- A task: to book a flight from Paris to Barcelona

- A post-testing interview to recall their experience and impression

- A SUS questionnaire

Participants

The participants included the following:

- Ten participants were recruited through a recruitment agency; a screener was prepared to select the correct users.

- A voucher was given to them as thanks for their time and participation.

- Five were clients, and the other five were clients of competitors.

Methodologies

All user testing sessions were video recorded with Silverback software. The screen of the iPad was displayed on the researcher's MacBook Air by using AirPlay, which enabled the researcher to record the MacBook Air screen with Silverback.

Notes were taken during the session. The notes were summarized in an Excel spreadsheet, and after the user testing, the video files were reviewed and added to that spreadsheet.

Thematic analysis was used to analyze the outcome of the session, with data being coded and organized into categories.

Similarities in themes could be identified across participants and across sections of the task.

Overview of the Findings

The findings included the following:

- Usability and functionality issues related to the search and the filters really need to be fixed, as the problem may cause users to quit the process (massive blockers).

- Price transparency should also be addressed, since it will make users leave the platform and go to the competitors.

- Visual design got positive feedback and was really appreciated by all the participants.

- We included why some users did not use the client's platform and what were some of the competitors' positive features.

- More specific testing should be done for the filters, especially those related to stopovers and flight length, and also to get more feedback related to insurance and luggage as a short flight task was not relevant.

Brief 7: Ops Portal

Many organizations work on a client-facing platform but tend to forget about the back-office users. We once looked at redesigning an internal process for staff, based on correspondence processes. This project was for a government organization in which correspondence arrived in several formats: paper letters, emails, and faxes. They used an old system, as well as other more recent ones. The process of correspondence involves many employees. High-level tasks included the following: opening letters, reading and uploading it on the system, allocating the request to the relevant department, technical team replies, verification, signature send the reply to the original sender.

Before planning to create a new correspondence system, the client wanted to conduct some user research.

After the meeting with the product owner, we understood the following:

- We had two weeks to make the discovery.

- Two researchers ware allocated to the project and were working directly in the agile team.

- The users are internal staff.

- People making a written question could be any citizen, politician, etc.

- The purpose is to create a better tool that facilitates the employee work and stop some back-and-forth, such as printing an email to scan it back into the tracking system.

Aims/Objectives

The project was in the discovery phase. The main aim of the project is to have a clear understanding of the current correspondence tracking process. The objectives included the following:

- To have a single platform that covers the whole process

- To draw an account of the current processes

- To understand who the users are

- To understand the user needs

- To create a better system that will optimize the processes and to be user-centered

Approach

We conducted some contextual inquiry in the user natural environment. We started by going to the mailroom and following several correspondences. We had to identify who all the users were through the process as well as where the correspondences were coming from.

This was to understand how users interact with the product during their daily work. Contextual inquiry/ethnography enables us to capture not only how they are using the current product but also to identify the other tools/products that they are using.

Most of the users were in the same department, but some were in different locations. We were shadowing members of staff who were involved in every step of the processes.

Participants

There were 15 to 20 participants, all of them internal employees.

Methodologies

Notes and pictures were taken throughout the contextual inquiry and feedback given by the users. The notes were summarized. We then started recording the processes and drew all the user journeys; we also made a list of all the user needs.

Overview of the Findings

The findings included the following:

- We could identify some frustration due to repetitive processes that could be optimized.

- We delivered all the user journeys through the process.

- We listed the user needs.

- We included issues that arose such as security, special correspondence, etc.

- We included different job roles through the processes.

Brief 8: Hardware and Software for Kids

A client was creating new hardware for children in China. The previous work for this hardware showed that the prototype was not meeting the user needs and it also had some ergonomics issues. The client had created an entirely new design, but some parts of the software remained the same. After conducting a first round of testing in a lab environment, the team implemented the recommendations. They were now ready to do another round of testing.

They wanted to test the product for a more extended period in the home of the users (natural family environment), instead of doing user testing sessions. They wanted to have the user use the hardware for a couple of weeks in their home to get some feedback based on real experience.

After the meeting with the product owner, we understood the following:

- We needed 12 participants.

- We had a tight timeline as the components needed to be ordered.

- The sessions would take place in Shanghai.

- Incentives would be given for both parents and children.

- We had some limitation in terms of the tools that we could use in China.

Aims/Objectives

The project was in the beta phase. The objectives included the following:

- To evaluate the suitability, the ergonomics, and the functionalities of the speaker as well as the content

- To evaluate parent and child behavior, motivation while unboxing, onboarding, as well as using the device over a two-week period

- To test the device in a natural setting for a longer period of time

- To evaluate the children's engagement

- To test the content and the hardware improvement

- To capture how often/how long users used the device and which feature they were using the most

Approach

The first part was a home visit that lasted between 60 to 90 minutes, with a native Chinese speaker (Mandarin) and researcher. The researcher introduced the speaker and to the family and informed them about the research process. The second part of the research was a diary study. The families were asked to use the device and to record the child's behavior through pictures and videos. Each family had a separate WeChat group to help the researcher extract the data. Parents could also report issues on WeChat.

After one week, parents were asked to complete the System Usability Scale questionnaire. In the second week, another piece of content was introduced to keep the children engaged.

Participants

Ten participants at the end took part in the research. They were all using the client's service. The children were between three and six years old.

They were recruited with the support of the client relationship team. An incentive was given to the parents and the children.

Methodologies

A contextual inquiry method was the first method used during the home visit (one when we brought the device and another one when we came to pick it up). This qualitative research approach is a face-to-face semistructured interview in the participant's/user's natural environment. A discussion guide was prepared and followed during the session.

A diary study was the second method used to collect data based on anthropology and ethnography. These approaches look at social phenomenon. This approach enables us to get insights from users while they are experiencing a situation. A study is longitudinal and captures temporal information. We asked the parents to take pictures or to video record when their child was using the device. We asked the parents to post the picture or video on WeChat (a Chinese version of WhatsApp). Every family had their own WeChat group. We extracted the videos and analyzed them using a thematic analysis.

For the contextual enquiry as well as for the diary study, we used thematic analysis to extract phenomenon and themes across participants. This has been done in relation with the different aspects of the device and its functionalities. Data was coded and organized into categories. Similarities in themes could be identified across participants, sections of the task, and user testing sessions.

Analytics

We tagged every device to find out which activity was most often performed and how often every participant used the device. We also looked at the SUS score.

Overview of the Findings

The findings included the following:

- We started identifying different personas.

- We got a better understanding of how the device integrated into family life.

- We got a better understanding of how a child interacted with the device.

- We also could see the features that were the most/least popular.

- We identified some usability issues.

- We re-evaluated the modifications done between the two rounds of testing.

Brief 9: Teacher New Training for New Responsibility Role

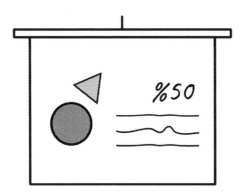

The department for education was creating a new role in schools, and it needed to create training for the role. Before starting the new training program, the department wanted a better understanding of who would be taking on the new role and how to best implement it.

After the meeting with the product owner, we understood the following:

- We planned to test it with around 20 participants.

- We had the data and support from the data analyst to identify the relevant participants.

- We had a researcher who could help for the fieldwork.

- We had a tight timeline with a holiday in the middle of it.

- We had access to participants across the country.

- We also needed to get some quantitative background research to move forward on the project.

Aims/Objectives

The project was in the beta phase. To create the best training and onboarding for the new role, it was important to have a wider understanding of the situation. We wanted to answer these questions:

- Who are the users?

- What type of organization is it?

- How many students are there?

- Do they already have something in place?

- How will they fit this new role in their organization?

- Who will be the best candidate with enough authority to make changes in their organization?

- Which type of training will be the most appropriate?

- Will they need different trainings depending on the size of their organization?

Approach

We started looking at the analytics of the schools in the country to identify the right audience. We decided with the team and with the social behavioral team which audience would be the most representative. Participants were recruited, and interviews were done in different schools across the country, such as small, medium, large, special education, academies, colleges, etc.

After conducting the interview and extracting the findings, we created a questionnaire survey based on the findings. This was to validate the findings with a larger sample size.

Participants

We identified the right sample (20 participants) that was the most representative. We recruited them and organized some visits in the schools, since teachers and head teachers were very busy and it was not possible to have them come to us.

We had 988 teachers who replied to our survey.

Methodologies

The interviews were audio recorded, and the content of the interview was transferred into an Excel document to be analyzed. We conducted a thematic analysis to identify systematic themes reflecting the participants' insights.

The findings were extracted to create a survey questionnaire, and we posted it on Twitter with the relevant hashtag. The data was analyzed and presented to the team.

Overview of the Findings

The findings included the following:

- The findings showed that more than 50 percent of the respondents were not aware of this new initiative.

- A large amount of schools already had something in place.

- The teachers who responded were interested in this new initiative.

- We had some directions regarding how they would like the delivery of the training to be done, the frequency, and who would be the best person in their organization to take on the role. We also had some open questions that matched some of the themes that we already identified from the face-to-face interviews.

Brief 10: Redesign of the My Account Section for a Gambling Website

The client was a gaming/gambling company that wanted to redesign the My Account section of its website. It needs some updating, since it looks a bit outdated, and some users even mentioned on the forum that it could be a good idea. Before starting the process to redesign the website, some research was needed to understand the user needs and identify which feature (if there was one) needed to be added to this section.

After the meeting with the product owner and the head of user experience, we understood the following:

- They already had some personas.

- A lot of research had been done on another part of the platform.

- They had a lab in-house.

- They had a data analyst team that could help.

- The design team could help with a mock-up at some point.

- The timeline was not set.

- There was no issue with the budget for recruitment and incentives.

Aims/Objectives

The project was in the live phase. The aim of the project and the objectives were to understand how the My Account section was used by users. Why did they use it? How often did they use it, and did they experience any blockers?

Approach

We started with the data analytics to get an overview of the activity on this section. Since we could see some inefficiency in the data, we started doing a discovery to understand why the section of the website was not working. In this case, there was very little activity in the deposit and withdrawal section.

We then tried to identify the other ways for users to deposit and withdraw money. We found out that operators from the call center could help users put money in or take it out from their accounts on the phone. After running a focus group with operators, we identified that removing an expired card was not possible, and when three cards were on the account, it was not possible to remove the expired one to replace it with the new one.

We also collected the data from call allocations, which helped us identify the correlation between the lack of traffic in the deposit and withdrawal area and the large volume of calls for the same purpose.

We also ran some focus groups with the end users, and they all said that they had issues with their cards.

Participants

The participants included the following:

- 24 participants took part in a focus group (8 per group); they were grouped by persona.

- There was one focus group with the operators.

- There were nine VIP users/clients.

- Participants were recruited with the help of internal marketing, customer relations, etc.

Methodologies

The methodologies included the following:

- Analytics (web activity)

- Focus group

- Face-to-face interview

- Analytics (call allocation)

Overview of the Findings

The findings included the following:

- To revisit the persona, we spoke with many types of users.

- We identified the issue, which was a massive blocker that was increasing dramatically the call volume at the call center.

- We moved through alpha, beta, and live to a solution. The design team, the developers, the financial department, and the legal department worked on a new process to add and remove cards, and it was then tested.

Summary

User researchers are exposed to a wide range of requests from their colleagues and clients. It could be performing a discovery, doing user testing, looking at analytics, creating a survey, etc. The main thing is to use the right method depending on the project. This chapter gave you ten briefs with some context. You can identify that although the process of conducting user research is the same, the research questions change, as does the research method to collect data. Still, the general process is the same.

- Getting a brief is essential.
- Refine the scope of the research in order to set up stakeholder expectations.
- Work with your stakeholders to draw up the research questions.
- Choose the relevant method to answer the research questions.
- Identify the right participants.
- Collect and analyze the data.
- Extract meaningful and actionable findings.
- Share your findings with your team and stakeholders.

Sample Script for User Recruitment

Hello, may I please speak to [**name**]? (if you have the name)

This is [**name**] from [**agency name**]. I am calling you on the behalf of [**one of our clients**]. They are looking for people who may be interested in participating in user research.

They are in the process of improving their tablet platform, and it is important for them that before they make any changes, they get the point of view and insight of people who are using it.

Obtaining feedback from you is one of the important ways we can ensure the development will meet the end-user requirements.

We are looking for people in the [**location**] area for face-to-face user testing who would be interested in spending 45 to 60 minutes taking part in this user testing and giving feedback of their experience.

[**Name of client/ company**] will use this feedback to help their team improve the customer/usability/user experience of their [**product**] experience.

Your input in this process would be highly valuable.

As thanks for your participation in this user testing session, you will receive a [**incentive**].

- **Does this sound like something you might be interested in?**

> [If yes, continue.]
>
> [If no, thank them for their time and terminate the call.]

253

© Emmanuelle Savarit 2020
E. Savarit, *Practical User Research*, https://doi.org/10.1007/978-1-4842-5596-4

- **The face-to-face interview session will take place in [location], [dates and time]. This session should take between 45 to 60 minutes. Will one of those days work for you?**

  [If yes, continue.]

  [If no, please ask if they know anyone who may be interested. Get that person's contact information, thank the respondent for their time, and terminate the call.]

Note   If you need to terminate the interview screening because the candidate does not qualify for the study, politely tell the candidate, "We already have enough people with this background, but thank you very much for your time."

If you have few minutes, I would like to ask you some questions to determine whether you are an appropriate candidate for this evaluation.

- **Do you have the time right now to answer a few questions?**

If yes	[Continue.]
If no	[Ask when would be a suitable time to call them back.]

- **Have you taken part in a marketing or user research study in the last six months?**

If yes	[Terminate the call.]
If no	[Continue.]

- **Could you please tell me which devices you own?**

• Smartphone	[Continue.]
• Desktop	[Continue.]
• Laptop	[Continue.]
• Tablet	[Continue.]

Which one?

iPad

Yes	[Continue.]
No	[Terminate the call.]
Nexus	[Terminate the call.]
Windows	[Terminate the call.]
Other	[Terminate the call.]

- **How often do you use your iPad?**

• Less than once a month	[Terminate the call.]
• Less than once a week	[Continue.]
• Between once or twice a week	[Continue.]
• Every day	[Continue.]

- **For how long have you been using your iPad?**

• More than a year	[Continue.]
• More than six months	[Continue.]
• More than a month	[Continue.]
• Less than a month	[Terminate the call.]

- **Do you shop online?**

• Yes	[Continue.]
• No	[Terminate the call.]

- **How often do you shop online?**

• More than once a month	[Continue.]
• Once a month	[Continue.]
• Once every three months	[Continue.]
• Once every six months	[Terminate the call.]
• Once every year	[Terminate the call.]

- **How do you pay for your purchases online?**

  - Card   [Continue.]

  - PayPal or similar   [Continue.]

  - Check   [Terminate the call.]

  - Other   [Terminate the call.]

- **How often do you travel?**

  - More than once a month   [Continue.]

  - Once a month   [Continue.]

  - Once every three months   [Continue.]

  - Once every six months   [Terminate the call.]

  - Once every year   [Terminate the call.]

- **How often do you book flights, weekend breaks, or holidays?**

  - More than once a month   [Continue.]

  - Once a month   [Continue.]

  - Once every three months   [Continue.]

  - Once every six months   [Terminate the call.]

  - Once every year   [Terminate the call.]

- **Do you book your flights, holidays, or weekend breaks online?**

  - Yes   [Continue.]

  - No   [Terminate the call.]

- **Which of the following sites you have used in the past?**

  - Air France

  - EasyJet

  - Ryanair

  - Go Voyages

  - ebookers

- Opodo

- Expedia

- Promovols

- Bravofly

- Easyvoyage

- Lastminute.com

- Liligo

- Voyages-sncf.com

- Je Réserve

- **When was the last time you booked a flight online?**

  - This week   [Continue.]

  - Last week   [Continue.]

  - Two weeks ago   [Continue.]

  - A month ago   [Continue.]

  - Three months ago   [Terminate the call.]

  - More than six months ago   [Terminate the call.]

- **Did you use your iPad to book?**

  - Yes   [Continue.]

  - No   [Go to the next question.]

  If no, when was the last time that you have booked a flight with your iPad?

  ....

  If they used their iPad several times   [Go to the next question.]

  If not   [Terminate the call.]

- **Which site did you use the last time you have booked a flight?**

  ....

  What is your profession?

  ....

  Gender

  - Female

  - Male

  Age group (we need a good age distribution)

  - < 25

  - 25–29

  - 30–39

  - 40–49

  - Older than 50

Sample User Research Consent Form

You have volunteered to participate in our user research testing program. To participate, please complete and return this consent form prior to the start. If you have any questions, please feel free to ask them.

Project Title

[**Name of the project**]

Invitation

You are being asked to take part in a research program to help design and create the new [**product**]. This research program has been mandated by [**funding agency**] and will be conducted and directed by [**your company**].

What Will Happen

In this study, you will be asked to interact with a prototype. The aim of the study will be to evaluate your interaction with the site. Some general questions will be asked about your online habits. You will also be asked to complete some tasks. There is no right or wrong answers; we are interested in your experience and how comfortable you feel using this website. Your feedback is important to us and will help us improve it.

© Emmanuelle Savarit 2020
E. Savarit, *Practical User Research*, https://doi.org/10.1007/978-1-4842-5596-4

Time Commitment

The study typically takes about 45 minutes.

Participants' Rights

You may withdraw from the study at any time throughout the research without explanation.

You have the right to omit or refuse to answer any question if it makes you feel uncomfortable.

If you have any questions regarding this research, we will answer them at the end of the session.

Cost, Reimbursement, and Compensation

Your participation in this study is voluntary.

Confidentiality/Anonymity

We will collect your name, age, email address, and telephone number for future contact as well as for a follow-up study where necessary.

Your data will be used to classify the feedback we obtain from the research undertaken. We may also reference you by your first name in our final report regarding any useful comments you may have made. Where necessary, please advise us, and we will be happy to anonymize your information in any reports distributed.

Video, audio, and screen activities will be used only for research purposes and will not be used in the public domain.

If we would like to use some of the recordings for conferences or publications, we will contact you and show you the recording to obtain your consent.

For Further Information

Our [**name of the researcher**] will be happy to answer any questions you may have. You may contact her at [**contact information**].

By signing below, you are agreeing that: (1) you have read and understoodthe consent form, (2) any questions about your participation in this study have been answered satisfactorily, (3) you are taking part in this research study voluntarily, and (4) you are waiving your right to request that we destroy any feedback received from you during the process.

_____

Participant's name (printed)∗

_____   _____

Participant's signature∗   Date

_____   _____

Name of person obtaining consent (printed)   Signature of person obtaining consent

Participants wanting to preserve some degree of anonymity may use their initials (from the British Psychological Society Guidelines for Minimal Standards of Ethical Approval in Psychological Research).

References

Amanfi, M. (2019) *The 4-Step Thematic Data Analysis with MAXQDA*. Self-published.

Barr, J. (2017) Why Most Corporate Software Stinks, and How Contextual Inquiry Can Improve It. Retrieved from: https://www.tandemseven.com/experience-design/how-contextual-inquiry-can-improve-employee-customer-experience/

Baxter, K., Courage, C. & Caine, K. (2015) *Understanding Your Users: A Practical Guide to User Research Methods*. Second edition. Morgan Kaufmann.

Bernard, H.R. (1995) *Research Methods in Anthropology*. Second edition. Sage Publications.

BPS (2014) *Code of Human Research Ethics*. Second edition. Retrieved from: https://www.bps.org.uk/news-and-policy/bps-code-human-research-ethics-2nd-edition-2014

Brooke, J. (1996) SUS – A quick and dirty usability scale. In: *Usability Evaluation in Industry*, Jordan, P. W., Thomas, B., Weerdmeester, B. A., & McClelland, A. L. (eds.). pp. 189–194.

Brown, G., & Yule, G. (1983) *Discource Analysis*. Cambridge University Press.

Chandran, S. (2018) User research within budget. Retrieved from: https://www.uxmatters.com/mt/archives/2018/06/user-research-within-budget.php

Coolican, H. (2018) *Research Methods and Statistics in Psychology*. Routledge, Taylor & Francis Group.

Corrall, M. (2016) How design mature is your organisation? Retrieved from: https://www.corralldesign.com/blog/2018/11/17/how-design-mature-is-your-organisation-1

Denzin, N.K., & Lincoln, Y.S. (2017) *Handbook of Qualitative Research*. Sage Publications.

DiSilvestro, A. (2018) The top 10 tools for getting an insight into your website analytics. Retrieved from: https://www.searchenginewatch.com/2018/06/04/the-top-10-tools-for-getting-an-insight-into-your-website-analytics/

© Emmanuelle Savarit 2020

E. Savarit, *Practical User Research*, https://doi.org/10.1007/978-1-4842-5596-4

REFERENCES

Drew, P. (2003) Comparative Analysis of Talk-in-Interaction in Different Institutional Settings: A Sketch. In: *Studies in Language and Social Interaction*, Glenn, P. LeBaron, C. D., & Mandelbaum, J. (eds.). Erlbaum.

Faulkner, L. (2003) Beyond the five-user assumption: Benefits of increased sample sizes in usability testing. *Behavior Research Methods, Instruments and Computers*, 35(3), 379–383.

Flaherty, K. (2016) Diary Studies: Understanding Long-Term User Behavior and Experiences. Retrieved from: `https://www.nngroup.com/articles/diary-studies/`

GDS (2017) GDS Service Manual: Finding participants for user research. Retrieved from: `https://www.gov.uk/service-manual/user-research/find-user-research-participants`

GDS (2018) GDS Service Manual: How the alpha phase works: Retrieved from: `https://www.gov.uk/service-manual/agile-delivery/how-the-alpha-phase-works`

GDS (2018) GDS Service Manual: How the discovery phase works. Retrieved from: `https://www.gov.uk/service-manual/agile-delivery`

GDS (2018) GDS Service Manual: How the beta phase works. Retrieved from: `https://www.gov.uk/service-manual/agile-delivery/how-the-beta-phase-works`

GDS (2018) GDS Service Manual: How the live phase works. Retrieved from: `https://www.gov.uk/service-manual/agile-delivery/how-the-live-phase-works`

GDS (2018) Understanding accessibility requirements for public sector bodies. Retrieved from: `https://www.gov.uk/guidance/accessibility-requirements-for-public-sector-websites-and-apps`

GDS (2019) What happens at a service assessment. Retrieved from: `https://www.gov.uk/service-manual/service-assessments/how-service-assessments-work`

Gibbs, G. (2018) *Analyzing Qualitatives Data*. Sage Publications.

Goodwin, C. Publications of Charles Goodwin. Retrieved from: `http://emcawiki.net/bibtex/browser.php?author=Charles+Goodwin&bib=emca.bib`

Gothelf, J. & Seiden, J. (2016) *Lean UX: Designing Great Products with Agile Teams*. O'Reilly Media.

GOV.UK (2019) WCAG 2.1 Primer. Checklist. Retrieved from: `https://alphagov.github.io/wcag-primer/checklist.html#checklist`

Guest, G.S., MacQueen, K.M., & Namey, E.E. (2012) *Applied Thematic Analysis*. Sage Publications.

Handa, A., & Vashisht, K. (2016) Agile Development Is No Excuse for Shoddy UX Research. Retrieved from: https://www.uxmatters.com/mt/archives/2016/11/agile-development-is-no-excuse-for-shoddy-ux-research.php

Hartson, R., & Pyla, P. (2019) *The UX Book: Agile UX Design for Quality User Experience*. Second edition. Morgan Kaufmann.

Hayes, N. (1998) *Foundations of Psycholog: An Introductory Text*. Second edition. Nelson.

Higginbotham, D. (2019) Graduate Scheme 2020. Retrieved from: https://www.prospects.ac.uk/careers-advice/getting-a-job/graduate-schemes

Higgins, T. (2019) Supreme Court hands victory to blind man who sued Domino's over site accessibility. Retrieved from: https://www.cnbc.com/2019/10/07/dominos-supreme-court.html

Ingold, T. (2017) Anthropology contra ethnography. Journal of ethnographic theory. 7, no. 1 (Spring 2017): 21–26. Retrieved from: https://www.journals.uchicago.edu/doi/10.14318/hau7.1.005

Jefferson, G. Gail Jefferson's Publications. Retrieved from: http://liso-archives.liso.ucsb.edu/Jefferson/

Kendon, A. (1990). *Conducting Interaction: Patterns of Behavior in Focused Encounters*. Cambridge University Press.

Kim, G. S. (2018) User Research Is 'Adulting' for Startups. Retrieved from: https://blog.prototypr.io/user-research-is-adulting-for-startups-d5c2269eadf6

Lang, J., & Howell, E. (2017) *Researching UX: User Research*. SitePointe.

Lawton, Henry, S. (2018) Web Content Accessibility Guidelines (WCAG) overview. Retrieved from: https://www.w3.org/WAI/standards-guidelines/wcag/

Lazar, J., Feng, J.H., & Hochheeiser, H. (2010) *Research Methods in Human-Computer Interaction*. Wiley.

Lyons, E., & Coyle, A. (2016) *Analysing Qualitative Data in Psychology*. Sage Publications.

Macefield, R. (2009) How to Specify the Participant Group Size for Journal of Usability Studies. Retrieved from: http://uxpajournal.org/wp-content/uploads/sites/8/pdf/JUS_Macefield_Nov2009.pdf

Mackey, A. & Gass, M.S. (2008). *Second Language Research*. Second edition. Routledge.

Marsh, S. (2018) *User Research: A Practical Guide to Designing Better Products and Services*. KoganPage.

Meiert, J. O. (2013) Revitalizing SUS, the System Usability Scale. Retrieved from: `https://meiert.com/en/blog/revitalizing-sus-the-system-usability-scale/`

Meyer, S. (2019) The 6 degrees of the UX maturity scale: How UX-ready is your company? Retrieved from: `https://www.testingtime.com/en/blog/6-degrees-ux-maturity-scale/`

McDonough, J. (1994). A teacher looks at teachers' diaries. *ELT Journal*, 48, 57–65.

Neilson, J. (2006) Corporate UX Maturity: Stages 5–8. Retrieved from: `https://www.nngroup.com/articles/ux-maturity-stages-5-8/`

Neilson, J. (2006) Corporate UX Maturity: Stages 1–4. Retrieved from: `https://www.nngroup.com/articles/ux-maturity-stages-1-4/`

Neuendorf, K. A. (2016) *The Content Analysis Guidebook (NULL)*. Sage Publications.

Nunnally, B. & Farkas, D. (2016) *UX Research: Practical Techniques for Designing Better Products*. O'Reilly.

Paul, G. L. (2010) Challenges to Leadership: Business Maturity. Retrieved from: `www.sydalco.com/white-paper.php`

Reeves, S., Kuper, A., & Hodges, B.D. (2008) Qualitative research methodologies: ethnography. *BMJ* 2008:337.

Reeves, S. Petter, J., Goldman, J., & Kitto, S. (2013) Ethnography in qualitative educational research: AMEE GuideNo 80. pp. e1365–e1379. Retrieved from: `https://www.tandfonline.com/doi/full/10.3109/0142159X.2013.804977`

Richie, J., Lewis, J., McNaughton Nicholls, C., & Ormston, R. (2014) *Qualitative Research Practice: A Guide for Social Science Students and Researchers*. Sage Publications.

Rubin, J. (1994). *Handbook of usability testing: How to Plan, Design, and Conduct Effective Tests*. New York: John Wiley & Sons.

Saldana, J. (2015) *The Coding Manual for Qualitative Researchers*. Third edition. Sage Publications.

Savarit, E. (2007) The Social Organization of Interactions Involving People with Aphasia. PhD Thesis. British Library.

Savarit, E. (2018) *How Is User Research Essential in Making e-Government Accessible to All? Human-Computer Interaction. Theories, Methods, and Human Issues*. Springer Nature.

Schegloff, E. Schegloff Publications Archive . Retrieved from: `https://www.sscnet.ucla.edu/soc/faculty/schegloff/pubs/index.php`

Schensul, J., & LeCompte, M. (1999) *Ethnographer's Toolkit*. Altamira Press. Retrieved from: `https://course.ccs.neu.edu/is4800sp12/resources/qualmethods.pdf`

Six, J. M. (2017) Establishing a UX budget. Retrieved from: https://www.uxmatters.com/mt/archives/2017/05/establishing-a-ux-budget.php

Six, J. M. (2018) Integrating User-Research Findings into Strategy. Retrieved from: https://www.uxmatters.com/mt/archives/2018/11/integrating-user-research-findings-into-strategy-1.php

Sola, D. & Couturier, J. (2014) *How to Think Strategically: Your Road Map to Innovation and Results*. FT Publishing.

Spanswick, R. (2019) Why Moderated User Research is Worth the Cost. Retrieved from: https://www.mindtheproduct.com/why-moderated-user-research-is-worth-the-cost/

Spinutech (2015) 7 Website Analytics That Matter Most. Retrieved from: https://www.spinutech.com/digital-marketing/analytics/analysis/7-website-analytics-that-matter-most/

Stockwell, A. (2016) How to adapt UX research for an agile environment. Retrieved from: https://uxmastery.com/how-to-adapt-ux-research-for-an-agile-environment/

Sweetwood, M. (2018) *Leader of the Pack*. Self-published.

Travis, D., & Hodgson, P. (2019) *Think Like a UX Researcher: How to Observe Users, Influence Design, and Drive Strategy*. CRC Press, Taylor and Francis Group.

Tullis, T., & Albert, B. (2008) *Measuring the User Experience*. Morgan-Kauufmann.

Turner, C. W., Lewis J. R., & Nielsen, J. (2006) Determining usability test sample size. In: *International Encyclopedia of ergonomics and human factors Vol. 3*, Karwowski, W., & Raton, B. (eds.). Second edition. Sage Publications.

For Further Readings

Find the best survey software for your business. Compare product reviews and features to build your list. Retrieved from: https://www.capterra.com/survey-software/

Why Accessibility? Retrieved from: https://dreamscapefoundation.org/why-accessibility/?gclid=CjwKCAiA27LvBRBOEiwAPc8XWRqecX4i7rVSXIJZ6OqzinxYlBhhZeNCT2kouw15zJp6zLSIe4qOhxoCITgQAvD_BwE

Disability fact figure. Retrieved from: https://www.scope.org.uk/media/disability-facts-figures/

Index

A

A/B testing, 170
Affinity diagrams, 183, 184
Alpha phase
    agile team, 35, 36
    collaborative work, 37
    designer, 36
    prototype, 37
    technical changes, 37
    trial-and-error process, 36
    two-week sprints, 36
Analytics
    analyze data, 125
    definition, 124, 152
    interpreting data, 126, 127
    present analytics findings, 128–132
    tools, 124
Anonymity, 260
Assisted digital technology
    difficulties, 213
    disabled people, 212, 213
    hearing impairment, 213
    nondigital users, 214
    recruiting participants, 214
    visual impairment, 212

B

Beta phase
    accessibility requirements, 39

product, 40
    team members, 38, 39
    test-improve-test-improve cycle, 39
Booking system, 191
Business maturity phases, 52, 54, 75

C

Card-sorting, 152
    analyzing/interpreting data, 147–151
    choose variant, 144
    closed card, 145
    create categories, 146
    definition, 143
    hybrid, 145
    IA, 143
    open card, 144
    presenting, 151
    recruiting participants, 146
    wording cards, 147
Closed card sorting, 145
Consent form
    anonymity, 260
    cost/compensation/
        reimbursement, 260
    invitation, 259
    participants rights, 260
    project title, 259
    time commitment, 260
Content analysis, 184

© Emmanuelle Savarit 2020
E. Savarit, *Practical User Research*, https://doi.org/10.1007/978-1-4842-5596-4

Printed in the United States
By Bookmasters